# The BossHole Effect™

## Managing People Simplified

## Dr. Greg L. Alston
### With Valerie R. Alston

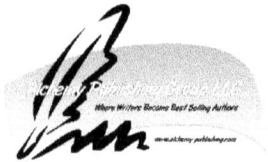

Alchemy Publishing Group, LLC
Reidsville, NC 27320
888-870-2519
www.alchemy-publishing.com

Juli Inhofer Editor

ISBN: 978-1-63297-003-9
Second Edition
Published in the United States of America

# Table of Contents

# Introduction: The BossHole Effect

"The leaders who work most effectively, it seems to me, never say I. And that's not because they have trained themselves not to say I. They don't think I. They think we, they think team. They understand their job to be to make the team function. They accept responsibility and don't sidestep it, but we get the credit. This is what creates trust, what enables you to get the task done." Peter Drucker Management Expert

Most people spend more time at their job than at any other activity throughout their adult life. These forty hours per week at work for fifty weeks per year for forty years is where they build self-esteem, make friends, and accomplish professional goals.

Unfortunately, it is also where they are forced to work with BossHoles and where we become discouraged by The BossHole Effect®. By definition, a BossHole is someone who acts like an ass and who happens to have the positional authority to impact your life. Other definitions of a BossHole taken from the UrbanDictionary.com include:

An employer of a particularly evil nature, completely devoid of empathy or concern for anyone else, the deadly hybrid of boss and asshole.

And my personal favorite: An asshole who is better at being an asshole than most other assholes.

1

The BossHole Effect® is the powerful capacity of a BossHole to suck the joy, energy, enthusiasm and greatness out of an organization. BossHoles don't just inhabit businesses. They can ruin non-profits, schools, sports teams, youth groups, homeowner's associations, church activities and just about any experience where a group of people gathers for a common purpose. BossHoles don't even have to be the official boss to exert their influence. The best of the breed require no official management or supervisory title.

A BossHole wields devastating negative energy, the metaphorical equivalent of a black hole caused by the implosion of a supernova. The gravitational forces created by a black hole are so strong that rays of light cannot escape their influence. The toxic anti-matter generated by a BossHole inflicts similar devastation on any workforce. Jeanna Bryner summarized University of Florida research in an article, "Abused Workers Fight Back by Slacking Off," in *Live Science* on October 8, 2007. This research demonstrated that workers with abusive bosses were five times more likely to slow down or make errors on purpose, six times more likely to hide from their boss, three times more likely to not give their best effort, and seven times more likely to falsely take sick leave.

The Gallup Business Journal published an article, "Many Employees would Fire Their Boss," on October 11, 2007. This research confirms the BossHole Effect®. The research indicated that 75% of workers report that dealing with their immediate supervisor is the most stressful part of their job; 24% would fire their boss if given the chance; 56% are unengaged and sleepwalking through work on any given day, and 18% actively undermine their team's efforts.

BossHoles create a multi-billion dollar negative drain on the gross domestic product of our nation and need to be eradicated to ensure our competitiveness in the global economy. But like the resilient cockroach this is easier said than done. The best we can probably hope for is to avoid contact with them whenever possible and to practice preventive maintenance. By not leaving anything around for them to feed on and by keeping some roach hotels strategically placed where they are likely to congregate, we should be able to minimize their presence. And when all else fails, we need to simply get over our fear of bugs and grind them under our boot heels one crunchy squish at a time. In modern guerilla warfare the weapon of choice is the improvised explosive device. (I.E.D.) In order to rid the world of business destroying BossHoles it is time to break out the B.E.D., the BossHole extermination devices.

Edmund Burke's famous quote is:

**"The only thing necessary for the triumph of evil is for good men to do nothing."**

Your challenge is two-fold. Do not tolerate BossHole behavior in others. And try not to act like a BossHole yourself. Everybody has bad days. Under stress everyone can occasionally behave inappropriately. But behaviors become habits and habits guide action. Don't let acting like a BossHole become a habit. BossHoles come in three general categories.

## The Complete BossHole

This jerk enjoys being a BossHole and thinks it is the right way to behave. He or she berates, abuses, demeans and belittles others like they are ignorant and unable to thrive in their absence. The only reason people work for this person is because they need the job and haven't found anything better yet. No one respects this arrogant punk and many secretly wish him/her harm. Everything this BossHole does is counterproductive to the development of an effective team. He/she will lie, cheat, steal your time, undermine the goals of the team, foster destructive habits and act smug about it.

## The Partial BossHole

This person doesn't want to be a BossHole, doesn't believe he/she is a BossHole, but commits just enough BossHole activities to ruin the effectiveness of his/her team. They usually have no idea that people think they are a BossHole. With guidance they can learn not to be a BossHole. Basically this person is trying to do a good job but just doesn't quite get it right. It is common for this type of boss to snatch defeat from the jaws of victory by routinely blowing the little things that matter.

## The Underground BossHole.

These people are scary dangerous because they pretend not to be BossHoles and only show their true colors when your back is turned. They smile to your face and shred you behind closed doors. They may not even officially be your boss but seem to feel that tearing you down will somehow catapult them past you in the organization. They will agree with you in private then sabotage your plans in public. If they do become your boss they inevitably become a Complete BossHole to you. While I hold out hope these people can change for the better, I have never personally witnessed such a conversion.

## *The Great Boss*

The Great Boss is by definition not a BossHole. In his book *Good Boss, Bad Boss,* Bob Sutton describes the qualities of a good boss. Based on his research he suggests that good bosses do certain things and behave in specific ways. Good bosses:

1. Consistently balance being too assertive with not being assertive enough
2. Possess the ability to stay after it until they get it done
3. Consistently produce small victories
4. Avoid undermining the dignity or authority of their subordinates
5. Protect their employees' ability to get their jobs done.

The difference between a BossHole and a Great Boss can be explained by asking three critical questions: Does your boss: Do everything possible to help you do your job well? Respect your dignity? Inspire you to excel at what you do?

I can tell you from my own experience that BossHoles can appear in your life at any time and without your permission. During one of my previous lifetimes I worked as a Regional Pharmacy Manager responsible for supervising over 100 stores for a major

West Coast drug chain. I went to work there because the boss was a good friend and a great person. However when the company was sold, a new leadership team came in and I was forced to work for one of the biggest BossHoles I have ever met. When I was writing the description of the Complete BossHole the image of this knucklehead was frozen in my mind. For the purpose of this narrative I will call him Dick.

Dick began his career on the East Coast and was hired to take command of our nearly 700 stores as the Vice President of Pharmacy Operations. On the morning of his arrival in Los Angeles I was asked to pick him up at LAX on the way in to the office. He was scheduled to hold an introductory session with the executive team. To describe Dick as abrasive would be like suggesting that 5,000 pounds of burning cow manure might have a slight aroma. Within five minutes of meeting Dick he had clearly indicated to me that I was to speak only when he gave me permission and that I had no idea how to run a drugstore. Within 30 minutes of meeting with the management team, Dick had accused one of the Regional Pharmacy Managers of being anti-Semitic and the rest of us were branded as morons.

I have never struck another person in anger in my life but I came as close as I have ever come when this BossHole chewed me out for ten minutes in front of my staff and customers at a new store opening. He had only known me for a few days so I couldn't possibly have earned this wrath. Regardless of the fact that Dick had no idea what he was talking about, and he had all of his facts wrong, to berate a supervisor in front of his subordinates is organizationally self-destructive. And I am not talking about a simple snide remark or a snotty comment; I am talking about a full-throated tongue-lashing accusing me of gross incompetence.

While this buffoon was wagging his finger and proving his complete BossHoleness in front of everyone, I could see through the double doors to the back of the stockroom. Each of our stores had a large heavy steel machine that was used to compact cardboard boxes into recycling bales, essentially a large trash compactor. I began having this out of body experience where all I could hear were the parental voices from the old Charlie Brown TV Specials bleating "Wah, Wah, Wah." Meanwhile I was daydreaming about the effect of this trash compactor on Dick in the event of a tragic "accident." I was imagining a scene from the 007 movie *Goldfinger*, when the villain crushed an uncooperative mobster in the automobile compactor at a wrecking yard.

This was one of the many times in my life that my wife has saved me from myself. Because just as I was beginning to rationalize that I could either do the crime and be out in seven years with good behavior, or knock this arrogant punk through a wall and insert my name badge in his forehead as I told him to take his job and shove it, I heard a voice in the back of my head. It was my wife saying, "He's not worth it and you can't quit." We were in the final days of completing construction of our new home and had not received the permanent financing from our construction loan yet. Changing jobs at that moment would have been a huge mess.

So I did what most employees do when they work for a BossHole. I shut down. I said, "Yassuh boss."

"Whadeva you needs, boss." I gave a big smile and counted the days until my loan was approved. The day after the loan was approved I began a new job with an employer that appreciated what I could do for them. And during the 30-45 days it took before I could leave, I supported my store teams but I spent most of the time laying the groundwork for my transition. Within 30 days of moving to my new employer I had successfully recruited several of the best pharmacy managers from my old company to join my team. We thrived while my old employer struggled. Now I don't typically gloat, but I will admit to a certain amount of vindication when Dick got himself thrown in jail for securities fraud a few years later.

If you work for a partial BossHole there is a good chance you can help them mend their ways. If you work for a Complete BossHoles then you either have to convince higher management to remove him or find a different job. Complete BossHoles rarely convert to Great bosses. My guess is that even when he gets out of jail Dick will still be a dick.

The last species of BossHoles I need to discuss is the Underground BossHoles. These people are devious and sneaky. They pretend to agree and be a good teammate but they save their knife wounds for when your back is turned. Sometimes it takes a while to smoke them out. You may never hear an unkind word directly from their mouths but they eventually leave their footprints in the sand somewhere. When they do you can plan your strategy to neutralize their impact. The thing that shuts them down more than anything is shining the light of truth on their behavior. They thrive like cockroaches in the dark of night. Once you turn on the kitchen lights they usually run for cover.

Hopefully none of you ever have to work for a BossHole. However, as in my case, that is not always under your control. You cannot control the twists and turns of life but you can control your own actions. In order to protect yourself from harm you must understand how to be a Great Boss so that you can help any supervisor you encounter learn to do the right things the right way to become a Great boss. More importantly, you can personally learn to be a Great Boss by reading the rest of this book.

The examples in this book are slanted towards the individual boss looking to own and operate his/her own business. However the principles and techniques that create team unity and effective action are the same whether you are applying them to your own business, a department within a larger business, or any team of people united in a common purpose. No matter what you hope to achieve someone has to set the tone and lead the charge. A Great Boss will always improve the performance of his team. So learn to be a Great Boss.

# Chapter 1: Why Read this Book?

"An organization's ability to learn, and translate that learning into action rapidly, is the ultimate competitive advantage." Jack Welch Former Chairman and CEO of General Electric

The overwhelming majority of people are mediocre. This is not a politically correct thing to say however, it is a statistical fact. Most people's daily actions hover within a narrow performance band around average. Statisticians call this distribution of behavior the Normal distribution and describe it as a bell shaped curve. What they mean by that is that sixty-eight percent of all performance falls within one standard deviation of average. If you are content to be within that sixty-eight percent then please don't read this book. Close it and now and file it away with all the other great books you have never read.

If you choose to continue reading then please understand that you do so at your own peril. The excuses that people typically use for failing to succeed involve reluctance to risk failure. This book shines the cold hard light of truth on how teams work and what causes them to excel. Once you understand the true drivers of championship caliber performance you will no longer be able to consider mediocrity acceptable. You will understand that failure is the stepping stone to greatness. You will become driven to pursue excellence. You will understand that you are in charge of your fate.

And you will no longer be able to use the excuses that you currently allow to prevent you from taking positive action.

And just in case you are wondering whether you have the ability to be great let me ask you a few questions. What percentage of companies do you think are great companies? What percentage of bosses are Great Bosses? What percentage of teams are great teams? Would you be happy if you were better than eighty-five percent of your competition? Well, all it takes to be better than eighty-five percent of your competition is for you to be a little bit better than average. Here is how I come up with that number.

If all competitors' performance is plotted on a graph and the graph is a Normal curve, the numerically average performance would be at the fifty percent mark. Statistically however, sixty-eight percent of the competitors would perform within one standard deviation of the average of fifty. Everyone within that performance band is statistically defined as average. Half of this sixty eight percent would be above fifty and half would be below the fifty mark. Adding fifty plus thirty four equals eighty four so if you perform at more than one standard deviation above average you will perform better than eighty four percent of your competitors. The good news is you don't have to become a superhero to become a Great Boss. All you have to do is transform yourself to be a little better than average and you will outperform eighty five percent of your competitors. This is a little bit of a geeky point but the math is correct. This book will teach you everything you need to know to rocket past average and become a Great Boss and the leader of a championship caliber team. You must learn to rise above the Bar of Mediocrity.

**The Bar of Mediocrity**[c]
**The Reason Why Above Average People Excel**

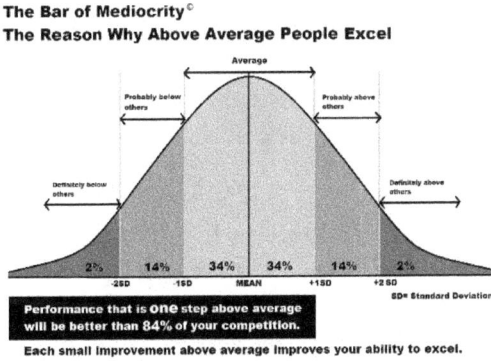

Performance that is **one** step above average will be better than **84%** of your competition.

Each small improvement above average improves your ability to excel.

An increasing body of research is suggesting that our educational system and self-esteem oriented culture have conspired to beat the creativity and love of learning out of a large share of our youth. "Helicopter parents" micromanaging their children's lives, a school system teaching to the test, and endless adult praise for participating rather than achieving, have generated a group of people who have always gotten the rewards without necessarily ever doing the work. When rewards are given without effort being required, the unmistakable message is that effort is not required.

Carol Dweck Ph.D., professor at Stanford University, is one of the world's leading experts on motivation. In her book, *Mindset*, she contends that people sabotage their own success when they operate with what she calls a fixed-mindset. People with this mindset believe that they are as smart as they are ever going to get and that you can't teach an old dog new tricks. They see no reason to put in effort to excel. After all, they get a trophy just for participating. If you have a fixed mindset then you have a choice to make. Get over it or abdicate your future to the efforts of others. The reality is that if you are not getting better at what you do, you are losing ground to your competition. And everyone is competing whether they choose to believe it or not. Sadly, until they acknowledge that they have something to learn, they won't.

If you see yourself as stuck where you are forever, I am sorry. That must be a miserable place to be. Successful people, however, don't believe that. They operate using what Dweck calls a growth mindset. These growth-oriented people believe that there is always something they can learn to do better.

This book is for people who want to be Great Bosses or learn to help their bosses become one. It explains the step-by-step process by which an individual can learn to be a Great Boss. Great Bosses build successful teams. Therefore, the focus of this text will be on the knowledge, skills, abilities and attitudes necessary to build a high functioning team. However, most small businesses start with a few employees and can't afford to take months to learn how to mold those employees in to an effective team. So the lessons presented here are designed to be implemented immediately by anyone who is willing to invest the few hours it will take to read this book.

Why should you care what I have to say? Because I have been where you want to go. I have worked in the corporate offices of three different large publicly traded companies, Sav-On Drugs, Thrifty Drug Stores and Smith's Food and Drug Stores. I functioned as a

Pharmacist, Pharmacy Manager, Training Manager, Marketing Manager, Category Manager, Pharmacy District Manager and Regional Pharmacy Manager. I was the first pharmacist in my graduating class to be promoted to pharmacy manager at a time when that mattered. I was the first pharmacist to become corporate training manager, marketing manager and then category manager for Sav-On Drugs at a time when that mattered. I was in the Executive Development Program with Jewel Companies, and I have spent more than 15,000 hours of my life in various meetings with executives in those companies.

Since leaving the corporate world, I have owned and operated several successful small businesses including a chain of Halloween shops, two drug stores, a medical supply store, a medical billing business and an Internet marketing company. I have unloaded trucks, vacuumed floors, remodeled stores, hired hundreds of people, fired more than I care to remember, worked 80 hours per week and agonized over every major decision.

I served on the local and national boards as a director and dedicated over 20 hours a week to coaching youth sports while raising two amazing kids with my high school sweetheart. I have experienced all the joys and sorrows of financing, building and operating businesses that depend on my efforts for their survival. I have lived through what works and what doesn't work in the small business world. I have paid dearly for my business education from the school of hard knocks. It has been a wild ride made palatable by the support of the woman I love. I wouldn't trade a minute of it for anything. But I wish sometimes that I had had some better advice from someone who knew better.

In 2007, I sold the retail businesses and embarked on a new career as an Assistant Dean and Associate Professor of Management at Wingate University School of Pharmacy in Wingate, North Carolina. Now I teach the next generation of pharmacists the management skills they need to thrive in the post Affordable Care Act world. And within 18 months of becoming an academic dean I won a national award for excellence from the teacher's academy.

During my business career I have supervised thousands of employees, worked for hundreds of bosses and battled organizational stupidity at every turn. I've worked with hundreds of managers, some of whom were brilliant, and I have worked with highly paid individuals who were dumber than a rock. I have seen what works and what doesn't work in the operations, human resources, marketing, distribution and purchasing departments.

I may be the only one in the country with such a unique resume of experience in management roles in a variety of settings. And even though everywhere I have been I have been successful, I possess no special intelligence. I have succeeded because I have been able to figure out what needs to be done and found a way to get it done. I have many faults but my singular unique talent is the ability to observe things that others don't see and to integrate those observations into effective action. This manifests in my being a voracious reader and collector of seemingly unrelated information that becomes the foundation for breakthrough ideas.

As a result of my experiences, I have developed a leadership philosophy that works. It works regardless of whether you apply it to your own business, a corporate position, an academic setting, a healthcare team or a sports team. It works because it is simple to explain and easy to understand. It works because it uses simple guidelines that can be applied to any setting. It works because it cuts out the crap and gets to the point. I believe in making everything as simple as possible but not simpler. I hope to describe this simple process of leadership in a way that you will be able to apply these principles to your own life, your own teams or your own business. My goal is to inspire you to translate what I teach into effective action. I learned a long time ago, as a corporate trainer that coming up with fancy slides and long-winded speeches is not a substitute for effective training. What real people in the real world want is knowledge and skills that they can turn into effective practices today.

Much has been written about the subject of leadership. My approach to teaching you to become an effective leader of others is driven by the fact that in most small organizations, the owner/operator or team leader must perform a variety of functions. The three functions that all successful leaders must perform are Coaching, Commanding and Creating an environment that engenders success. These three simple steps to becoming a Great Boss – Coach, Command and Create - provide the backbone for effective and actionable leadership of any enterprise that seeks to be good at what it does, whether it is made up of players, pharmacists, doctors, executives, plumbers or teachers.

If you have not had the opportunity to manage others in a competitive environment, you may not understand what I mean. So let me finish this introduction by giving a couple of examples from my fast pitch softball coaching career to illustrate the impact a single leader can have on the outcome of a team. I know that some of you may not enjoy sports analogies, but they are hard to avoid when you are discussing teams because they provide such a target rich environment of examples. If you don't get sports then just bear with me as I will mix in examples from community practice pharmacy as well.

In the first case, imagine that at the very early stages of the championship season, in the first practice game prior to the start of tournament competition, you have 15 players on your team. As this first practice game gets into the late innings with a tie score, your team comes up to bat with the winning run on second base and two outs. One of your new players is the next scheduled batter. As the coach you have two options: You can let this new person take the at-bat and try to drive in the winning run or substitute a hitter that you know much better to attempt to drive in the winning run. Imagine the impact of this decision, not on the outcome of this individual game, but on the development of this player as a productive member of your team by the end of the season.

If you pull this new young lady out of the game for a pinch hitter, in the first practice game of the year and do not give her the opportunity to drive in that run, you will have created doubt in that player's mind. She will begin wondering: "Does my coach think I am not good enough? Why does my coach not trust me to perform? If my coach is not going to allow me to try to hit in a practice game when it doesn't really matter, when is he ever going to allow me to hit when it does matter?"

The potential positive impact of a trusted familiar player coming up, getting a base hit and winning the game versus the negative impact of demoralizing, demotivating and disengaging that new person from your team effort, is something that a good leader must consider. If you win the meaningless game and end up destroying the relationship with the new player, have you really helped your team in the long run? If you communicate to your new player, "I don't believe in you. I don't trust you," how will that impact her desire to excel in the future?

The net effect of this decision to send in a pinch hitter for the new player is that the coach is arbitrarily determining the value of that new player to the team without ever giving the player the opportunity to prove what she can do. In that scenario, the typical reaction of the player is to withdraw and stop trying. Her response is usually, "What difference does it make if I work hard if he's not even going to let me have the opportunity?"

Now consider a different way to handle this scenario. Prior to the critical at-bat, you call a timeout. You go up to the young lady and say, "You know what? I don't care whether you get a hit or you don't. What I need you to do is get a good pitch and hit it hard somewhere, and then we'll just see what happens. Don't worry about trying to knock in the run. Just relax. This girl throws 80% of her pitches on the outside corner. I want you to take that outside pitch and just hit me a nice sharp ground ball up the middle."

That same young player will now get back into the batter's box with an entirely different mindset than the player who gets pulled for the pinch hitter. She will think; "The coach trusts me enough to let me try. He knows that I can't control the outcome. Even if I don't get a hit, as long as I have a good at bat, coach will be happy." The real upside of this leadership strategy is that the coach has let the player determine the level of success she achieves by her own performance. If after a sufficient number of at bats the player cannot get the job done, that player may rightly find herself cut from the team. But in the second scenario the player's performance has determined whether she stays on the team, not the coach's arbitrary guess. Her performance, rather than an artificial decision by the coach, has determined the outcome. This is one example of how the leadership style I will explain to you can have a huge impact on the psyche of your team.

I'm going to give you the other instance where I think a small effort to apply effective leadership can have a huge impact on the character, morale and engagement level of your team. Imagine that your team is participating in a team-building event at an outdoor challenge course. Your team is faced with a task. The task is a 15-foot-high wall. Your job is to get all 15 players plus coaches over that wall in 10 minutes. The rules are that you can't use any tools other than yourselves. You can lift each other. You can throw each other. You can do whatever you want but you have to get people over this wall. The task is crystal clear - get your team over that wall.

Imagine that the team is focused. They give a full effort, but they cannot get that last person over the wall and time expires. You are left with options as the leader of this team. The first option is that you can shrug off the failure and give up. You as the leader of that group can say, "Okay, we didn't make it. Let's go on to the next station. Let's go try the next event."

Another option is to refuse to accept defeat. You can look your team in the eye and say, "I don't care about the time limit. I don't care about the next event. We're not leaving here as a group until we get over that wall. If we have to stay here the next 10 days, we're going to figure out a way to get this done."

Consider what these different options communicate. In the first case, "We didn't make it. It's okay. Don't worry about it. We tried." In the second scenario, "We're not leaving until we succeed. We don't care what the rules are about an artificial time limit. We're not leaving. We're not giving up until we succeed as a team."

It is a single leadership choice but a huge difference in the long-term impact on your team attitude and chemistry. Real leadership occurs at unexpected times, and the moment must be seized when it occurs. You must learn to find these teaching moments, develop an effective strategy to capture the good lessons and then model the values you are trying to instill in your team. Leadership is less about grand strategies and Harvard business plans and more about leading by example. You will show leadership by acting like a leader. If you will do that, you can turn any group of teammates into an effective, powerful, successful organization.

**"Executives owe it to the organization and to their fellow workers not to tolerate non-performing individuals in important jobs."** Peter Drucker, Management Expert

So come with me on this journey towards learning to be a Great Boss by building a team that will achieve excellence. The process is the same regardless of what you want this team to accomplish. Whether you wish to build your own business, develop a product team within your existing organization or develop a competitive youth sports team, the process is the same. It doesn't matter whether you want to be the primary leader or simply help others get the job done. There is a process that will lead to success, and this book is designed to help illuminate that process.

**Don't become a BossHole and never forget that friends don't let friends become BossHoles.**

# Chapter 2: The Power of Three

**"Things should be made as simple as possible, but not any simpler." Albert Einstein**

I believe in the power of three. Three is a magic number. It is a prime number. It can't be divided by any other whole number. Three just seems to resonate with the universe. With most problems in life, there are only three unique alternatives. You can: Do the right thing, do the wrong thing or do nothing. The brain is made to remember things that come in threes. A list of three is not too short and not too long. You can remember three names like Groucho, Chico and Harpo or Tinker to Evers to Chance. Three is just an easy number of things to remember.

Retail purchasing patterns demonstrate that three is a good number of choices. If you have a good choice, a better choice and a best choice, that is really all you need. Adding 10 additional choices doesn't increase the number of sales; it complicates the decision and actually decreases the number of people who buy, because they become confused. Three is a powerful tool to use when discussing how to turn decisions into actionable plans.

With most decisions you have to make, there are really only three options. Is what I'm about to do going to: Make it better, make it worse or have no impact? The key to being a Great Boss is the action you take once armed with the answer. If you are about to do good then do it. If you are about to do harm then don't do it. And if it doesn't really matter then you need to stop wasting your talent and work on something that will improve your performance.

So if you want to be an effective leader, if you want to build an effective team, and if you want to be able lead that team to achieve great things, there are really only three modes of behavior that you must incorporate into your leadership style. Great Bosses do these three things well, BossHoles do not.

## *Coach Mode*

The first is Coach Mode. A coach is somebody who takes each individual teammate and builds her knowledge, skills and ability step by step until she can become an effective and productive member of the team. Great Bosses are good coaches, BossHoles are not. If you want to be an effective coach, there are really just three skills you need to master. These are:

1. **Vision**-understand what the real end game is. Know where you're going and what you're trying to accomplish. Have a clear vision of your destination.

2. **Flexibility**-customize directions for each individual teammate. Some teammates need a pat on the back. Some need a kick in the butt. Some need a day off. Some need to work through it. Some need praise. Some need to be left alone. Equal treatment for all does not mean identical treatment for all.

3. **Process**-apply the right technique at the right time to get the best performance possible. People learn by building patterns of success. They get discouraged when they have patterns of failure. The job of the coach is to know how to balance the failure, which identifies the

need for improvement, (competence builders) and the success, which demonstrates the results of the applied effort (confidence builders). The goal of a coach is to make a teammate better than she could have become on her own. This is worth repeating. Your role as the coach is to help each teammate become better than she would have become if she had never met you. (Become a force multiplier)

## *Command Mode*

The second mode required for effective leadership is command. Any well-constructed team can do many things without micro-management. Nevertheless, there are times when a leader has to make a difficult intra-competition decision for the team to get the best result. That is the act of commanding. Great Bosses give orders when they need to but let their subordinates struggle when they need to. BossHoles micromanage and interfere with good decision making processes. In order to be an effective commander, there are three skills that you need to master.

1. **Intention**- knows the command intent of the mission. Understands, not the written orders or the vocalized orders, but the true nature of the orders and the plan.

2. **Recognition**-recognize the game that you're in. Let me use a major league baseball example. In the course of a 162-game season, in about a third of the games your team will lose by a wide margin. In a third of the games you're going to flat out crush the other team. And in the last third of the games the battle will be hotly contested down to the last pitch. Either team can win or lose. You

must learn as the commander to recognize where you are in the battle, what type of game you're in, and make decisions appropriate for the game at hand.

3. **Timing**-make the right call for the right conditions. It is not always obvious to the players who should be doing what. The team is so involved in playing the game or running the business that they may not be able to step back and recognize what today's strategy for success is. A good commander applies the right burst of leadership at the right time to get the desired outcome. Every second guesser can analyze an act after the play is over, but only Great Bosses can execute the right action in real time.

## *Create Mode*

The third mode is Create. A leader must learn to create an environment in which the team can thrive. A leader must learn to motivate and to inspire the team to rally around the cause. A Great Boss will inspire the team to succeed now and in the future. Inspiring the team to succeed is entirely different from ordering the team to succeed. Great Bosses know how to actively engage each teammate in creating excellent performance. BossHoles routinely create an environment that stifles performance. I wholeheartedly agree with the U.S. Army field manual FM 6-22 statement on leadership. In order to be a good leader and inspire others to excel you must master the three skills of providing:

1. **Purpose**-keep the team focused on the long-term vision for success.

2. **Direction**-inspire the team to excel by engaging them in the mission.

3. **Motivation**-energize the process of success.

Deciding how problems are approached, how adversity is dealt with, how effort is rewarded and how freedom is granted will either energize or deflate a team's competitive fire. Great Bosses inspire their teammates to engage in and believe in the team's mission. People join good organizations, but they quit bad bosses. The modern employee does not want to be managed, she wants to be inspired. Long-term successful businesses employ people who are inspired by the mission, and then give them the freedom to be successful.

Great Bosses create an environment that allows teammates to thrive in their roles. They do that by driving all-important decisions as close to the bottom of the organization as possible, and then empowering teammates to make those decisions without fear of punishment. A BossHole paralyzes the creativity and resilience of the team by hoarding decision making power closer to the top of the organization, thereby communicating to the entire team that teammates are not empowered to act without fear of reprisal.

The reality of the 21$^{st}$ century is that no one person can know enough about everything to be able to micromanage a complex system. The distribution team, the customer service team, the sales team and the support team all know more about what they need to do than the executive team. In healthcare, the physician is the diagnostician, the pharmacist is the medication expert, the nurse is the care expert and the support staff does the billing. A n organization that gives every element of the organization a seat at the decision making table will make better decisions. And this remains true when you play all of those roles yourself as a solo entrepreneur. You must learn to change perspectives based on the task you are trying to complete.

This does not mean that each stakeholder needs to have an equal vote in the process. The executive team still needs to exercise their Command role, but the process for making high quality decisions, that is, decisions most likely to work and achieve the desired result, require an open airing of the real issues. Far too many teams attempt to avoid conflict at all costs. But teams without friction never get better. They never push each other to make mistakes they can learn from. To create the sharpest edge and most durable sword the blacksmith applies heat and hammer. A Great Boss knows when to pound and when to polish to get the best result.

In addition, the Internet has drastically altered the competitive landscape. Everyone in the world competes with everyone for virtually everything. Both good news and bad news travel fast. Somewhere in the web cloud someone is fact checking and criticizing everything that every organization does. The only recourse to avoid damaging blows to a company's reputation is to be above reproach. Any deceit, failure, dishonesty or mismatch between a company's stated values and performance will be reported and available for the world to see.

No team leader can escape this reality, and the pressures are even tougher when you are the executive, financial, marketing and sales director for your own firm. You can't be an expert in everything you need to know; therefore, you have to build a team you can trust to help you get where you want to go. For those of you who have never been involved in corporate decision-making, this may seem a bit theoretical. So let me explain what I mean when I say that keeping the decision making power too high in the organization can have disastrous results.

In 1981, I worked as the marketing manager for professional services for Sav-On Drugs, which was a 150-store drugstore chain based in Southern California. The company had just been purchased by the Jewel Corporation, which also owned Osco Drugs in the Midwest. Jewel was an amazing organization with an inclusive management style that fostered good decision-making skills in its executives.

Jewel was a people-oriented organization and published a manifesto titled the *Jewel Concepts*. Jewel believed in the "first assistant" philosophy of management. Each manager was to see himself or herself as serving the people he or she managed. A manager would be the "first assistant" by making personal contact and taking personal interest, solving problems, suggesting solutions and using flexibility in order to best serve the employees' concerns. I still keep a copy of the *Jewel Concepts* in my desk today. Jewel believed in empowering workers to do their jobs well. They believed that it was each employee's obligation to passionately argue for what they thought was right when it was time for input and to passionately support the team decision once it was time for action, regardless of whose idea prevailed.

Jewel Corporation methodically reviewed the Southern California and Chicago markets and the culture of both Sav-On and Osco and made the strategic decision to not merge the two companies into one operating unit. Their argument at the time was that each company had powerful strengths in its core competencies but enough differences that they would be more likely to prosper with their own brand in their home markets. Jewel successfully operated multiple store brands such as Star Markets, Buttrey Food Stores, Osco Drug, Jewel Food Stores, Sav-On Drugs and White Hen Pantry in diverse markets across the country. In 1984 American Stores, which owned the PayLess drugstore chain, purchased Jewel. American Stores, directed by L.S. "Sam" Skaggs, had a much more autocratic decision-making style. Basically, Mr. Skaggs got what he wanted, and very few people in his organization had the authority to disagree with him.

In this case, he wanted a national chain with one nameplate. By 1986, Osco was declared the brand, and all of the stores in Southern California were re-labeled at huge expense to be called Osco. The results in the Southern California marketplace were disastrous. After losing sales, market share and goodwill at alarming rates the brand was switched back to Sav-On in 1989[2]. This enormous expense in signage, repainting and loss of market share all could have been avoided if the company would have listened to their Southern California employees and customers and heard their legitimate concerns.

And here is the key point I am trying to make. Mr. Skaggs was not a stupid man. He built a huge business empire from humble beginnings. He was by many measures a tremendous success. But even a person with his track record doesn't know everything. His inability to create a culture where dissent was encouraged cost his company millions of dollars. It is easy when you are having a run of success to fall prey to the arrogance of believing that you as the leader are the source of that success. Great leaders succeed when they surround themselves with good people and let them do their jobs.

General George S. Patton, whose Third Army accomplished incredible battlefield success during World War II and was instrumental in the Allied victory, said this best when he stated, **"Never tell people how to do things. Tell them what to do, and they will surprise you with their ingenuity."**

He also crystallized what I call the essence of great leadership when he said, **"Lead me, follow me, or get out of my way."**

# Chapter 3:  The World Is What It Is

**"The superior man understands what is right; the inferior man understands what will sell."  Confucius**

Leadership can be either a positive experience, when a leader leads in the right direction, or a negative experience, when the leader takes his team down the wrong path. One of the primary causes of leadership failure is ignoring reality. Great Bosses lead in the right direction, BossHoles lead in the wrong direction. Many leaders fail to participate in the real world. They somehow view their organization as different and not subject to the "laws" that drive effective organizations. They ignore the marketplace and doom their organization to extinction, because they refuse to learn the lessons the market has to offer.

Alan Leighton, Chairman of the Royal Mail, described an interesting process where bad leaders unintentionally undermine their own organizational objectives. My guess is that a significant percentage of these bad leaders are BossHoles. According to Leighton, organizations fail because of four self-inflicted wounds.

1. **Complacency**: When an organization becomes complacent, it stops innovating, which sows the seeds of its demise.

2. **Complexity:** An organization begins to fail when it adds increasing layers of complexity to everything it does. These layers detract from the mission and

divert resources to checklist monitoring. The mission begins to get lost in the details.

3. **Market insight**: Imagine a critical military installation that fails to provide an adequate radar shield around its base. How would the soldiers know they are in danger from an incoming threat? The worst risk an organization can take is to not have an advanced early warning system in place that identifies approaching danger.

4. **Arrogance/Entitlement:** When an organization begins believing that it is entitled to exist regardless of performance. It begins losing touch with the reality of a dynamic marketplace.

Many small business people make the mistake of trying to emulate the actions of the high profile corporate types while trying to run their own small businesses. The reality is many high-paid executives run their companies into extinction because they are bad leaders. Many executives are paid millions to do a horrible job. Let me give you a real example from one of my past lives.

In 1991, I was responsible for preparing the operations budget for the 660 pharmacies in the Thrifty Drug Chain, based in Los Angeles. The chief executive at the time was Elvira (named change to protect the guilty) who had recently joined the company from a clothing operation. Elvira was the lady who hired Dick, the Complete BossHole, I described in the introduction to this book. Not surprisingly Elvira was an arrogant BossHole herself. She was not as abrasive as Dick but had her own unique spin on BossHole stardom.

Elvira fired every executive who had experience running drugstores and brought in cronies who would not challenge her ridiculous attempts to redefine a drugstore chain as a fashion boutique. She began a scheme to add clothing and fashion items and remove merchandise categories that essentially define the drug industry. At that time I was responsible for preparing the detailed budgets for all stores. After painstakingly researching the sales and margin trends in each store and building them into an operational budget for the entire chain for the next year, my V.P., Dan and I presented this budget to the executive budget committee. The events of that meeting are burned into my psyche.

This BossHole lady demanded that we raise our pharmacy gross profit margin from 25% to 45% by raising our prices. Then, after Dan explained that prescription pricing was regulated by insurance contract, and we could not raise our prices, she never spoke to him directly again. We were all sitting at the table and she would look at me and say, "Tell Dan that we are not going to accept those numbers." To say that this BossHole acted like a childish brat would be like suggesting that the Titanic experienced a minor fender bender in the North Atlantic. Needless to say she fired Dan who was a Great Boss and replaced him with Dick, the Complete BossHole. So for those of you who believe in the law of attraction I believe this is evidence that BossHoles attract other BossHoles.

This executive was paid several million per year to plunge the company into bankruptcy. A company that had been purchased for $850 million dollars six years earlier was within days of Chapter 7 liquidation when it was sold to an investment group for $247 million. And that is not the worst of how that company behaved. At a time when the pharmacy department generated over 50% of the sales and 60% of the operating profit of the company, the Vice President of Human Resources stood up in front of a meeting with all of the District Managers and Regional Pharmacy managers present and told the following joke:

> "What is the difference between a catfish and a Pharmacist? One is a scum sucking bottom dweller and the other is a fish."

Imagine the impact this type of attitude had on the pharmacists who were working there. When this negative attitude was backed up with policies and decisions that aligned with this callous disrespect for the profession of pharmacy, it is no wonder the company struggled to succeed. Believe me when I say that you do not want to emulate corporate behavior just because some BossHole gets paid a lot of money. Great leadership is based on aligning the vision, mission and values of an organization with its practices. Therefore, in the cases I just explained, the leadership was the opposite of good. So let us talk about the world as it really is.

You can reminisce about how the world used to be. You can lament about how the world should be. Nevertheless, the world is what it is. Most people do not have the ability to alter the world. However, at some point in your lifetime, you will be presented with the opportunity to make a difference. You will have to make a choice to rise to the challenge of that opportunity or shrink from it. Your attitude will largely determine your perception of that opportunity. It is through this perception that you filter your actions. The result of your actions can alter your small portion of the world. If this alteration is sufficiently compelling, it may gain traction and ultimately change the world.

Actions taken without good purpose are unlikely to produce changes that create value. Actions guided by noble precepts have the power to triumph. However, success will depend on good people making good things happen. There are only three kinds of people in the world:

1. Those who make things happen
2. Those who watch things happen
3. Those who have no idea what just happened.

Of the people who make things happen, there are two types: people who make good things happen and people who make bad things happen. For the world to improve, we must have people who make good things happen. If you are someone who has no idea what happened, you have only three choices in life:

1. Get educated about the right thing to do;
2. Get educated about the wrong things to do; or
3. Remain ignorant.

People who get educated about the right thing to do no longer have 'no idea' what happened. People who get educated about the wrong things to do will cause bad things to happen. People who remain ignorant either have no capacity to learn or choose not to. The clear pathway to success is to get educated about the right things to do and to move from a position of ignorance to being able to at the very least, watch things happen. Once you internalize the right things to do, you can begin gathering the skills you need to make things happen. If you are someone who has watched what happens without taking any action to improve things, then you have only three choices:

1. Learn to **become a leader** to make good things happen;
2. Learn to **become a follower** to help good things happen;
3. **Do nothing** and help prevent good things from happening.

Improvement requires positive action. Doing nothing is a choice, a choice driven by fear of failure or sloth. Inaction by default assists those that prevent good things from happening. To make good things happen, you must understand who makes things happen. It is individual leaders who make things happen. If you are a person who makes things happen you can:

**1.** Become a force for **improvement;**
2. Become a force for **destruction**; or
**3.** Waste your talent on **indifference.**

Not everybody has the capacity to be a great leader; however, everybody has the choice to participate in improvement or destruction. Obviously, the pathway to success is to become a force for improvement. You can become a positive force by playing your part as either a leader or supporter of good things. If you do not help those around you make good things happen, then you are part of the problem, not part of the solution. If you are not part of the solution, you risk becoming irrelevant.

There is a world of difference between being a good manager and being a good leader. Managers manage people, resources and processes to improve productivity. Managers take the system a leader has developed and attempt to operate that system at high levels of efficiency. Leaders set the course; managers keep the team on course. In a small business, the owner/operator will frequently be the leader of the business and the manager of the process. But as the organization expands, the management role can be delegated to others.

To explain the difference in the two roles is to consider a major project such as the construction of the transcontinental railroad. Leaders made key decisions regarding the route, the type of trains, the method of construction and the resources needed to complete the project. Managers hired and fed the crews, supervised the work, paid the employees, procured the materials and made sure the tracks were completed on time.

If managers had simply been told to build 3,000 miles of railroad track without a map to tell them where to place any of it, the results would have been disastrous. The map and the general plan had to be decided by leaders. The details of the day-to-day management of the operation required onsite problem solving by engaged management, adapting the plan to the terrain of reality. In your quest for knowledge and leadership skills, you have been focused on what you need to know. Now is the time to think about how you are going to translate those skills into action.

To be a Great Boss, your actions must produce good results. To produce good results, you must understand what good results are and have an effective plan to achieve excellence. To achieve excellence, you must be able to manage the challenges that you face throughout the rest of your career. Possessing all the knowledge and skill in the universe will do no good if you are unable to apply the knowledge and skills when needed. Effective action is the essence of good leadership. You can learn to be a Great leader by mastering the three C's: Coach, Command and Create.

# Chapter 4: The Process of Leadership

**"Leadership is the art of getting someone else to do something you want done because he wants to do it." Dwight D. Eisenhower**

We can summarize the process of effective leadership that leads to being a Great Boss rather than a BossHole by asking four questions.

1. What is the process by which you take a group of individuals and mold them into a highly competitive team?
2. How do you get a group of people to get what needs to be done completed in the right way, in the right time?
3. How do you get that team to be a group of people that energize you and are fun to be around?

There are techniques that work. There are also techniques that don't work. One of the more interesting phenomena I observed as a youth sports coach was that a lot of people don't know how to lead or how to be a positive role model. Many coaches were people who were fairly arrogant. There are people who think that because the name on their hat and their shirt matches, that they are in fact a genius. Almost always, their selfish motives provide the exact opposite of a positive experience for many kids. I learned that if your heart is not in the right place, you are by nature a bad leader.

One of the most exhilarating experiences I had as a leader of a nationally ranked fast pitch softball team was bringing together a group of kids that these geniuses didn't want on their teams, and then beating the genius' team on the field of play. My teams would compete and beat the best teams in the country because we played the game the right way.

If a leader's process is driven by ego and the need for recognition, it can succeed in the short run, but will likely fail in the long run. If you try to rush the process and take shortcuts to success, chances are you won't succeed. What I'm going to try to explain is what I believe are the essential elements of developing and understanding a good process by which you can create a highly competitive team that you will be proud to lead.

There are really only three challenges you will need to master to become a Great Boss.

1. **Clarity:** have a clear view of what it takes to win. Clearly articulate what you want your team to do.

2. **Process**: develop a process that builds patterns of success and does not produce fear of failure. Think twice before you speak because your words will plant the seeds of either success or failure in the mind of others.

3. **Mindset**: internalize and accept that you can only control things that you can control. You can control your team's efforts. You can control their practice habits. You can influence their attitude and effort. You cannot have any impact on the weather, the umpiring or who shows up to play against you. Worrying about things you can't control will keep

you from performing to the best of your ability on the things that you can control.

Focusing solely on outcomes, winning, getting the hit and driving in the run can create a cycle of failure when you don't get the hit or win the game. Focusing on the process being done correctly, focusing on the approach to your at-bat, focusing on playing the game the right way inspires self-confidence, controls what can be controlled and will eventually succeed based on the inspired and self-directed effort of your teammates.

Let me give you a classic example from the world of coaching. Every parent wants to be a good parent. But every parent secretly yearns for their child to be the star of the team. Since for most kids this will never be true, this sets parents up to be disappointed. This disappointment can spill over into creating a negative pressure on their child to control outcomes they cannot control and lead to hurting the very child they are trying to help.

Consider this situation. Little Susie is unprepared for the game, does not put in the required work on her hitting during the week and fails to listen to the scouting report on the opponent for this game. The coaching staff knows the opposing pitcher well. She thrives on a spinning drop ball below the knees but she does not throw hard enough to throw a fastball past a good hitter. The team strategy is to not swing at drop balls early in the count in order to make her throw a fastball that is hittable.

In every at bat, Susie swings at a first pitch drop ball. In her first at bat, she hits a dribbler up the third-base line that goes for a base hit. In her second at-bat, she pops up to second base, the second baseman loses it in the sun, and it drops for a base hit. On the third at-bat, she hits a three-hop roller that kicks off the second base bag and rolls into the short outfield for a base hit. She's three for three, batting 1000. Her parents are ecstatic. After the game, they're bragging about how Susie went three for three in the game.

Susie's teammate Janie works hard and practices every day in the batting cage. She studies pitching patterns and listens intently during the scouting report. During the same game in Janie's first at bat, she has a ball inside off the plate called a strike, and another ball above the letters that the umpire calls a strike. She's down 0 and 2, fouls off four to five tough pitches and not trusting that the umpire won't make another bad call on her, she leans in on a pitch 2 inches off the outside corner and smokes that ball into deep right-center field. The right fielder makes a running, leaping catch up against the wall. In her next at-bat, she works the pitcher to a 3-0 count and then drives a fastball deep to right field that is caught for an out. In her third at-bat, with the bases loaded and two outs, she works the count to 3-1 and then she smokes a ball to the left-center gap. The center fielder leaps in the air and catches the ball. She's out. She goes 0 for 3 in the game.

Janie did exactly what she was coached to do. She exhibited an outstanding at-bat against top pitching and took the exact right approach, hitting the ball on the button each time, but she went 0 for 3. If her parents are upset that she didn't get a hit, what have the parents taught this young lady by their reaction to the outcome rather than process? Would they not be saying that training hard and doing everything right doesn't matter if you don't get a hit? In Susie's case, if her parents are happy, because she went 3 for 3, what have they taught their daughter? Would they not be teaching her that she can be lazy and ignore her coaching as long as she gets a hit in the scorebook?

Lionel Tiger in an article "Dominance in Human Societies" in the journal, *Annual Review of Ecology and Systematics*, Vol. 1 (1970), states that a typical baboon troop member glances at the Alpha male to watch for cues about how they should act every 20-30 seconds. And much like baboons I believe this hardwired biology also extends to human employees. They watch the leader for verbal and nonverbal cues all day long every day. This can be extremely annoying when you are the Boss but it is never going to change. The behavior you model speaks louder than any words. And it is critical that you behave as if they are always watching you because they are. And with the magic of smartphones they are also probably recording you.

As the coach of those two kids, I would talk to Susie about how to take a better approach in that big at-bat. I would express my disappointment at her lack of preparation. I would encourage her to follow our hitting plan. She was lucky this time, but over time she is going to have more success if she would put her work in and follow the scouting report.

I would make a point of telling Janie, and everybody within earshot, that she did exactly what she was told to do, and I am amazingly proud of her efforts. She did exactly what she was taught to do. Consequently, even though we didn't get the results out of it in this game, there is going to come a game, a time, a situation when, because of her preparation and focus and doing what she was taught to do, we're going to win, because she will be prepared.

In Carol Dweck's book *Mindset*, she describes her research on Growth and Fixed Mindset that I mentioned earlier. People with a fixed mindset hold the erroneous notion that their value is directly a result of their innate ability. Thus their self-esteem is riveted to their performance. Failure at a task causes them to question their ability. Each new challenge therefore becomes another new opportunity to be found worthless. Faced with this stress their performance suffers and they resist doing anything they don't already know how to do well.

Adopting the growth mindset refocuses these challenges as opportunities to grow and get better. A Great Boss makes sure to coach and create in a way that fosters a growth mindset in their employees. They do this by praising proper effort, tactics, and techniques used by players like Janie. And they encourage the Susie's of the world to work harder at becoming better.

Consider your business for a moment. Are you teaching people to perform the right process? Are you satisfied because you're getting okay results? Are you impeding your team's progress? BossHoles that scream and yell because a teammate makes an error rarely earn the respect of their team. Coaches that praise the right effort, the right dedication, the right focus and reward those efforts with the play time are building a pattern of success that will help their team succeed in the long run. Success requires preparation. It requires focus and dedication. And it requires controlling the only things you can control, which are your attitude and the quality of your preparation.

Consider a teammate who disregards your signal to bunt and decides to swing away. That teammate is lucky enough to get a hit and win the game, but she has done so by ignoring your signs from the coaching box. How would you handle that situation? In other words, what is the process by which you want to operate? Given the scenario I just described, you have three possible choices. You could decide that the player was being defiant. You could say, "Nine times out of ten times the smart play is to make that bunt, and your defiance of me indicates that you don't want to be a part of this team."

You could decide that the player could be right. You could say, "I trained you to be an RBI machine. I don't know what the hell I was thinking asking you to bunt. That's on me. We had talked about the approach in this situation. We talked about the kind of pitcher we were up against, and our strategy was that if I got you in that situation, you were going to drive the ball and that you were going to attempt to drive in the run, and I messed up. You were right."

Or you can chicken out and do nothing. This will leave everybody else to decide whether the player was right or the coach was right. But remember they are all watching for your reaction. The process of developing an effective team means you have to understand what it takes to prepare to win a big championship game that won't be played until several months from now. And your team is watching what you do and what you don't do. Weak BossHoles just pretend that nothing is wrong and avoid taking any action.

Far too often in the pharmacy setting I have seen managers ignore bad behavior because they didn't want to take the time or effort to deal with it. But all persistent behaviors are rewarded, and if you are not stopping bad behaviors when they occur, you are rewarding it in the eyes of your team. Either you build trust, engagement and support, or you build doubt. You build patterns of success or patterns of failure. The process that is most likely to succeed is building patterns of success from a foundation of solid and predictable strategies. You can't try to win the game. All you can do is play your best and let the game develop. Winning is not everything. How you play, how you prepare, how you compete is equally important and much more under your control than the breaks of the game.

One team I coached that best exemplifies the power of teamwork was a group that did not win the national tournament. Going into the tournament, we were considered no more than 30th best out of 84 teams. We didn't have a lot of the big-name players, but we had an assortment of kids who were battle tested and believed in each other. We had only two players who had been to Nationals before, a lead-off hitter with no speed, one legitimate pitcher, and a player who had just joined the team batting third. We did not have the talent of most of the other teams and far less experience. But what we did have was a group that worked their tails off three days a week to get better. They played without fear. They supported each other. They played hard but didn't take themselves too seriously. And they had amazing resiliency.

We were sailing through the tournament undefeated until we played the game from Hell. I think that every player on the team made at least one error and we turned what should have been a close game into a resounding defeat. It was one of those weird games where nobody could do anything right. Unfortunately, this knocked us into the loser's bracket and matched us against the team that was ranked number one and had just lost the winner's bracket semi-final. If we allowed this disastrous breakdown to affect our mood or allowed the fear of facing the best team in the country to create a fear of failure, we would have been done. This was that critical moment when the Boss could inspire with a well-chosen comment or demoralize the team with negativity.

The coaching staff huddled with the players after the game and rather than chew them out for playing poorly simply said, "We want to thank you guys for getting us to this next game because this is the one we have wanted to play all year. No one expects us to beat this next team, we've got nothing to lose, let's go give them the fight of their lives." Our kids played free and loose. We scored first and kept the pressure on the whole game only to lose at the very end due to a freak play where the home plate umpire called a ball fair that the third base umpire called foul creating confusion that allowed the winning run to score. We outplayed them, we outscored them we just got a bad break and lost the game. But this bunch of misfits finished 9th in the nation. It was very cool.

The process of building a successful team is very simple. You need a clear view of what it takes to win; you must have a process that builds patterns of success and not "fear of failure"; you must understand that you cannot control what you cannot control. Effort and execution are more important than short-term results. In the long run, the best results are most consistently achieved by superior preparation. Every player on your team has a role to play in every game, in every situation. For some it's the lead role, for some it's the support role, but for players to feel like they are a part of the team, they need to feel that their role is useful, is valued and is necessary to the success of the team.

The history of sports is stuffed with examples of weaker talent "on paper" winning the championship over a more famous team. The New England Patriots with young Tom Brady beat the Rams and Kurt Warner's greatest show on turf in 2002. The 1988 Dodgers beat the unbeatable Oakland A's with a bunch of guys that weren't considered good enough to be on the A's team, and the light hitting San Francisco Giants in 2012 swept the Detroit Tigers and their dominant pitching. There is a reason that some teams succeed despite having inferior talent. When the team is properly constructed and everybody on that team has a role, understands it and performs it, then that team will be competitive. The process of building that team is no different - whether you're building a softball team, a baseball team, a staff of people to run a drugstore or a clinical outpatient care team. Each player on the team wants to know three things:

1. That what they do is **important**,
2. That they're **good at it** and
3. That the **boss values** their contributions to the team.

Perhaps one of my most cherished memories as a coach occurred when a group of young ladies won the national tournament. One of the players was not anywhere near the best athlete on the team and was struggling to win a spot in the starting lineup. About two-thirds of the way through the season, it was pretty obvious that there were better players at every position that she wanted to play. But understanding the fact that there could quite possibly be a time when I would need her to help us win, I needed to find a way to keep her prepared and ready. My strategy with her was to find what she could do well and put her in that position to be successful. I made a deal with her. I asked her to prepare to do one single thing. I told her that when I bring her in to hit, if she will hit me a ground ball to the second baseman, she would help me win games. Because if I had a runner on third base with less than two outs, and she could drive in that run consistently, I knew I could use that skill to help the team win. As luck would have it at the national championship tournament, I was able to find eight situations where she could step up and perform her role. In those eight at-bats, she had six RBIs, two hits and drove in key runs that led us on to victory. Even though she was not a starter and even though she was not a star on the team, she played a key role in helping our team win that tournament. The look of joy and satisfaction on her face at the end was worth all the time and effort it took to get there.

The process of successful leadership requires the Great Boss to understand how to get the players to engage in the mission, to put in the work, to do the preparation and to have the attitude and effort to be successful. You won't always win, but you'll earn respect. In business, you won't always win but you must earn the respect of your customers. Great businesses succeed by doing the little things exceptionally well. If you give a full effort in the right way, about the right things, you will succeed in the long run. Learning how to coach, command and create the environment in which your team can succeed is a crucial element of your team's success. Great Bosses learn how to create this positive environment; BossHoles do the exact opposite.

# Chapter 5: Knowledge, Skills, Abilities and Attitudes

**"Nothing can stop the man with the right mental attitude from achieving his goal; nothing on earth can help the man with the wrong mental attitude."**
**Thomas Jefferson**

Attitude is the trump card for every hand you are dealt in life. But attitude alone cannot get the job done. For anyone to succeed they must have at least a minimal ability to perform. So what is the difference between knowledge, skills and abilities? Knowledge is what you know. Let me use baseball as an example. There are three outs in an inning. You run the bases counterclockwise. If a player catches the ball in the air, it's an out. If I hit a ground ball to the shortstop, and he throws it to first base before I get there, it's an out. These are all bits of knowledge about the game of baseball. Building on your knowledge and little bits of things you know, you can tie this knowledge together to perform a skill. A skill is something you can do. Baseball skills are things like hitting, throwing, fielding and running the bases. Ability is something entirely different. Ability is an amalgamation of knowledge and skills honed over time to develop the talent to piece all that together and perform an act. The ability to play the game of baseball involves the skills of hitting, running, throwing and catching. It involves the knowledge of the rules of the game: how many outs, how many innings, the infield fly rule, but ability can only be accurately assessed by observing performance. The ultimate assessment of ability is can you actually do it?

You can know the game, you can run really fast, you can catch, you can throw, you can hit, but the most important measure is what happens when I put you in the game? If you can't do any of these things in the right place at the right time, you cannot integrate your knowledge and skills into ability. You may run really fast; however, you don't get started until it is too late. You may hit the ball a long way, but you strike out too much. You may throw to the wrong base or fail to play solid defense. Essentially, if you don't help us win games when you are on the field, then you are not performing the abilities we need for success.

Having the talent is not the same as performing the ability. The concepts are often misconstrued as interchangeable. The ability is a complex development and integration of multiple skills and bits of knowledge to produce a result. We can practice and train on knowledge and skills, but the only way you can verify that a person with talent has the ability is to put the person in the real situation and see if they can do it. Talent comes from DNA and is about potential. Ability comes from practice and is about performance.

You can take a course on customer service management and how to be nice to customers. However, until you're standing at the counter the day after a four-day weekend when two other people have called in sick, we won't know if your lessons have translated into performance. When you are trying to calm an angry mob of customers as you get their orders filled on time, you begin to understand the real ability to deal with pressure while maintaining composure. Thus, it is important that good leaders understand that knowledge is something that employees can read about, skills are something they can practice, and ability is the real world performance of a complex process. When you understand these distinctions, you will begin to comprehend that there is a process that goes with developing ability. Sometimes teammates flash good skills in one area, but fail to demonstrate the overall ability you need.

Far too many coaches make the mistake of predicting ability from skills. Let me give you an example: You're having infield practice. We're going to hit ground balls to the third baseman, then we're going to hit ground balls to the shortstop, then the second baseman, then first baseman and so on. The player standing at third base knows, "Okay, it's my turn. Coach is going to hit the ball to me. I get two to the backhand, two to the forehand, two that I have to charge." The skill of fielding backhand, forehand and charging ground balls is complex. However, the ability to do it in the real game is different than the simulation in practice, because the player knows in advance where the ball is going to be hit in practice. If I know the ball is going to be hit to my backhand, I can cheat to my backhand. If I know it's going to be hit to my forehand, I can step to my forehand. In the game you don't know where it's going to go. If you're an observant person, if you can read the flight of the pitch and gauge the swing of the bat, you can get a jump on the ball that a more physically gifted player may not. The skill of recognition and reaction is different than the practice skill of fielding a ground ball. People can be better at reading and reacting than they are at fielding ground balls in practice. However, the real ability that matters in a real game, in a real situation, in a real at-bat is the ability to recognize what's going on, get in the right place and get the play made.

Quickness is a mental skill, speed is a physical skill. The fastest person in a foot race is not necessarily the quickest reactor to the real world. Players with slow foot speed but fast reaction times can be where they need to be and make the play based on that skill, rather than their foot speed. So making decisions from practice time only and trying to apply it to real-world game situations is not a 100% accurate science. I would submit that in the real world it's probably less than 50% accurate. One dispensing technician can be really fast but not very accurate while another is slower but never makes an error. One may get distracted easily and only complete 60 orders a day while the slower one stays on task and completes 75 orders per day. If you are going to be a Great Boss, you have to make sure that you are paying attention to the right stuff. BossHoles pay attention to the wrong stuff. Therefore, three keys to developing a successful team are:

1. **Teach** the foundational knowledge
2. **Develop** their skills
3. **Reward** ability by giving your players the opportunity to demonstrate that they can perform in the real world. Don't make the decision for them. Let their play dictate the decision.

Now, of course, there is a standard. Somebody that can't catch and can't throw at all is not going to be able to perform the ability because they could get hurt. You're not going to put somebody who is clueless in the middle of your business process and ask them to

56

perform a complex task when they can't even get to work on time, carry on a conversation, follow procedures or even be accurate. What I'm talking about here is when you have reasonably competent individuals and you are trying to decide who is best at the job. It's very easy to make decisions, but it's hard to make the right one. The best way to make that decision effectively is to give them the opportunity to show what they can do and let the best rise to the top.

Great Bosses understand the foundational knowledge the job requires, the skill set the job requires, the process for training those skills, and then lets people play their way onto the field by demonstrating their ability. The BossHole thinks differently. The BossHole makes personnel decisions based on bad data, with no process, and penalizes failure to the point that no one is willing to try to succeed. A BossHole's idea of training is to find someone who already knows how to do what he wants done. The leadership challenge is deciding which attributes the players on your team need to possess and which attributes you do not want them to possess. In order to determine which knowledge, skills, ability and attitudes you wish to encourage, there are three things you need to know:

1.  What are the key personal **attributes of success**? Know them, internalize them, and recognize them within the behavior of other individuals.

2.  What are the key **negative attributes** that prevent you from succeeding and damage your team? Know them, internalize them, recognize them in others and determine whether those attributes are something that can be changed or not.

3. How to identify and **separate** out the **good** people **from the bad** people and the people that possess the likelihood of becoming good.

I believe there are only three kinds of people in the world:

1. There are **good people** who wake up every day meaning to do good things, planning to do good things, trying to do good things. Sometimes good people do bad things, but most of the time they do good things.

2. There are **bad people** who wake up every day with bad intent. They intentionally do bad things. They have no desire to do good things. Sometimes bad people do good things, but usually, when a push comes to a shove, these bad people will do the wrong thing at the right time

.

3. There are people who **haven't matured** yet. They might be predisposed to good or bad behaviors based on those with whom they spend time. Nevertheless, they can still be redirected and taught to do the right things.

To be a Great Boss you're going to have to learn to identify whether someone is a good person who occasionally does bad things, a bad person who occasionally does good things, or somebody who can be redirected. When you're assembling a team, you want good people who do good things. You want to eliminate bad people even though they occasionally do good things, and you have to be willing to help develop people who have the potential to be good but haven't realized it yet. Developing employees in a work situation is really no different. The skills you are looking for in a good employee are the good habits that you expect all good employees to have: honesty, punctuality, they get along with others, they work as part of the team, they take direction, they're capable of learning, they have a positive attitude, they treat your customers well. These are all things that good employees do.

On the other hand, there are bad employees. They can't seem to make it to work on time. They call in sick a lot. They can't get along with your other employees. They sabotage and undermine your policies. They fight with other employees and customers. They work behind the scenes to behave dishonestly. The real key to successful leadership is the ability to recognize who is good and reward them, who is bad and get rid of them, and who is capable of learning and train them.

There are job-specific skills required of whatever job you're hiring for. You have to know what those skills are. You have to know the character traits for which you are looking and you have to be able to recognize the difference between a good person and a bad person. More damage is done to an organization by keeping a bad person on the team than is ever done by any other cause. When you have a bad person on your team and you fail to get rid of them, you are communicating to your entire team that bad behavior is acceptable. What are you communicating when even a bad employee still gets a raise? What are you communicating when an employee who doesn't show up on time and fights with everybody doesn't get her hours cut? What are you communicating when a bad employee, who fights with customers and disregards policies, doesn't get terminated? You are subtly indicating that good behavior has no reward and that lousy behavior is acceptable. One bad employee not dealt with can destroy the entire fabric of a good team.

Here is the biggest real world twist on this problem. Sometimes that bad employee is capable of really good things. In bursts they can perform dramatic feats and appear to be really good and then turn around and undermine everything you do. There is no more important attribute in a teammate than character, and a bad person's behavior indicates they are a bad person at their core. There are several different types of pencil and paper tests that can give you clues about character, but the ultimate test shows up in behavior, and usually in behavior that is detrimental to the team. Bad people are typically selfish and this manifests under stress as selfish behavior. And the result of selfish behavior is predictably bad for the team.

Researchers have laid the groundwork for defining what the good attributes of employees are. Seligman and Peterson, in their book *Character Strengths and Virtues* defined the 24 character strengths that successful people possess. These Include:

1. Zest: approaching life with excitement and energy; feeling alive and activated

2. Grit: finishing what one starts; completing something despite obstacles; a combination of persistence and resilience

3. Self-control: regulating what one feels and does; being self-disciplined

4. Social intelligence: being aware of motives and feelings of other people and oneself

5. Gratitude: being aware of and thankful for the good things that happen

6. Love: valuing close relationships with others; being close to people

7. Hope: expecting the best in the future and working to achieve it

8. Humor: liking to laugh and tease; bringing smiles to other people; seeing a light side

9. Creativity: coming up with new and productive ways to think about and do things

10. Curiosity: taking an interest in experience for its own sake; finding things fascinating

11. Open-mindedness: examining things from all sides and not jumping to conclusions

12. Love of learning: mastering new skills or topics on one's own

13. Wisdom: being able to provide good advice to others

14. Bravery: not running from threat, challenge, or pain; speaking up

15. Integrity: speaking the truth and presenting oneself sincerely and genuinely

16. Kindness: doing favors and good deeds for others; helping them; taking care of them

17. Citizenship: working well as a member of a group or team; being loyal to the group

18. Fairness: treating all people the same; giving everyone a fair chance

19. Leadership: encouraging a group of which one is a valued member to accomplish

20. Forgiveness: forgiving those who have done wrong; accepting people's shortcomings

21. Modesty: letting one's victories speak for themselves; *not* seeking the spotlights

22. Prudence/Discretion: being careful about one's choices; not taking undue risks

23. Appreciation of beauty: noticing and appreciating all kinds of beauty and excellence

24. Spirituality: having beliefs about the higher purpose and meaning of the universe

Their research indicates that the character traits most directly predictive of academic success are: zest, grit, self-control, optimism, gratitude, social intelligence, and curiosity. I believe that these same character elements are the best predictors of whether or not an employee is a good person who you want to hire, retain and promote, or an employee that you need to ask to leave your organization. And the beauty of this list and the way the terms are described is that you can rate the terms based directly on observable performance. It is rather easy to read the item and check whether the person is or is not performing the desired behavior. The alternative to the good characteristics you hope to find in your employees are the negative attributes that you can use to identify the bad employee. After 35 years of managing thousands of employees I have created a list of the top ten common negative behaviors by a team member that can undermine the success of the team. These are:

1. Negativity
2. Non-excused absences
3. Failure to complete work/assignments
4. Disrespectful or abusive behavior
5. Uncooperative or domineering behavior
6. Failure to give best effort all the time
7. Failure to provide constructive feedback
8. Whining
9. Poorly prepared for work, meeting.group activity
10. Subversive behavior.

A Great Boss should always expect the best behavior from their team and each member of the team at all times. By clearly stating and modeling these behavioral expectations, your team has the best shot at being productive and successful. Your strategy for success as a Great Boss has to be to create an environment where the good character traits become the culture of your organization, and the negative attributes get surgically eliminated quickly. You can easily identify these attributes by observing people's behavior. Knowledge and skills are important, but abilities and attitudes are critical. Character and attitude are much more important than skill once you have determined they have mastered the basic requirements of the job.

As a college professor, I frequently remind students that getting good grades in school is a skill. It does not correlate with the ability to do anything useful. The artificial world of academia is much like the practice field in baseball. It's a limited set of options presented in a limited way in a very controlled environment. The ability to read, react and respond in real time is much more important than the ability to get good grades. History is full of examples of people who couldn't stand school that went on to tremendous career success. It is also full of examples of people that did very well in school that end up disgraced because of illegal and unethical behavior.

To illustrate the negative consequences one selfish, unethical person can have on a team I will describe an example from my coaching career. The biggest disappointment and biggest failure I had as a coach was my 18 and under team. We had a tremendous amount of ability and a great group of players. Toward the middle of the season, our best all-around player, clean-up hitter and a real emotional leader on the team, had the opportunity to move up from the 18 and under team to our gold team. We let her take that opportunity but it left a big hole in our lineup. We found a young lady and brought her onto the team who could hit the ball a ton, had tremendous focus at the plate, and I truly thought we were blessed to bring this person on board so late in the season. Unfortunately, I found out too late that her character would prove to be our demise. Right after qualifying for the national tournament this young lady began to cause trouble.

First she was caught shoplifting in a department store and then money began disappearing from other players' purses during practice. Despite a fair and equitable rotation, she began to complain about playtime and started to undermine our team unity. This boiled over in a key game during our national tournament run where she made two errors that cost us a game and knocked us out of the tournament. This marked the only time in a ten-year period that my team failed to finish in the top ten as we landed 13th. If I would have cut her loose at the first sign of trouble, I believe that team would have won the championship. We had all the right players and talents to get the job done. What we had was one wrong player who undermined it all.

My fear of losing the good things that she did bring – big hits, a lot of home runs - kept me from doing what I knew was right, which was to eliminate the cancer from my team. I will never make that mistake again. The two critical questions to keep in the back of your mind as you are choosing new team members are: Do I want to be around this person every day? And, is this person somebody I'm proud to know? If the answer to either question is no, keep looking for someone better.

In addition, a Great Boss hires based on the answer to three questions:

1. Does she **possess the skills** I need?
2. Will she **mesh well** with my team? and
3. Can she do **what** needs to be done **in the way** that I need her to do it?

If one piece is missing, the employer and candidate are not a match. As a Great Boss, if you compromise your standards because you have a hole to fill, you'll end up paying for it later. It is always better to wait to find the right person rather than hire the wrong one.

Great Bosses create the environment in which their team can thrive. They provide encouragement and foster a team-centered approach. A BossHole does the exact opposite. A bad team rots from the head down. Allowing lousy behavior to exist destroys the team. Swift removal of negative players inspires the team. Success is a process tested daily. Not doing your part is not acceptable. Whining about it is not acceptable. Sabotage is not acceptable. Failure to cut out cancer will allow the cancer to grow. If you had a tumor growing on your lungs, would you sit back and watch it and hope that it goes way and doesn't hurt you? Or would you diagnose it, cut it out and treat it? Evidence based medicine tells us that catching it early and eliminating it is the best way to have long-term health. Ignoring it will devastate your body, sap your strength and jeopardize your health. Ignoring bad behavior is one potential strategy for dealing with problems, but it's potentially a lethal one.

# Chapter 6: Awareness of What's Important

"You can't connect the dots looking forward; you can only connect them looking backwards. So you have to trust that the dots will somehow connect in your future. You have to trust in something - your gut, destiny, life, karma, whatever. This approach has never let me down, and it has made all the difference in my life." Steve Jobs

In this context, what I am talking about is: Are you aware of what's going on in the marketplace, and do you even know the right things to pay attention to? If you are in the process of designing a business model to be competitive in the marketplace, there are quite a few things you need to know about what's going on. Certainly you should be able to survey the landscape of competitive offerings, know who is out there, what business they are in and what approach to the customers they're using. You should be able to craft a business plan for yourself that allows you to develop a competitive advantage, or at least a marketing advantage to be able to attract and retain customers within that marketplace.

In the context of leadership, market awareness really comes down to; do you know what you need to be paying attention to in order to get your team to reach its goals? A Great Boss will constantly assess the mood of the team and analyze the impact of his or her actions. Are your actions helping the team get closer to its goals or are you preventing the team from reaching its goals?

This is not a matter of intent; it is frequently unintentional. Sometimes your frustration, your personal biases or stress manifest in your actions. When you take an action that is detrimental to the team, you need to own up to that and reverse the consequences of that action. That's part of being a Great Boss. BossHoles rarely admit they made a mistake. Is what you're doing positively impacting your team? If it is, do more of it, but if it isn't, do less of it. The next thing you have to be aware of is the ability to focus on the real performance issues, the critical things that actually help your team succeed. These are not the same things that the textbooks might tell you, and you may not find them in your company policies and procedures manual. They are, however, the true drivers of success.

Let me give you an example: In one of my previous lifetimes, I functioned as the seasonal buyer for Sav-On Drug Company. One of my responsibilities was to prepare the fall season tradeshow. We would bring in all of our vendors, all of our store managers and assistant managers and layout all the ad programs for the upcoming season. This show allowed the store managers to see what we were going to run on ad, see the programs we had developed, meet with the vendors, see and touch the product, order what they needed for their stores and then place those orders and have them put in the queue to be delivered. It was a three-day event at a major convention center, with 500 attendees, setting up booths and running a basic trade show.

My contractual responsibility for the job was a typical 40-hour work-week, 8-5, but clearly with this kind of event, those hours were not sustainable. The week before this trade show event, I would usually spend about 24 hours a day on site between the hotel, the convention center, work, last-minute coordinating, problem-solving, and meeting with the show decorators. In other words, doing all the things that needed to be done to make sure that this kind of event came off without a hitch. Getting the order guides prepared and setting up the electronic order systems takes a tremendous amount of time and effort.

Typically by the time the event was completed, I had spent close to 110 hours in the previous seven days at work. I barely had gone home to see my family, and I was emotionally drained and exhausted. After three days away from home, I staggered back into the office on Thursday night and sat down with my boss. I told him, "You know what? I'm not coming in tomorrow because I'm exhausted, and I put in a zillion hours this week and I'm dead tired and I'm going to go just go home and sleep all day." My boss looked at me and said, "You can't do that. If I let you not come in tomorrow, I'd have to let everybody not come in tomorrow and that wouldn't be fair."

And my comment was, "You know what? Anybody that has put in 110 hours in the last seven days should have the right not to come in tomorrow. I know we're on salary but come on. I just pulled off this huge event which was a rousing success, and you're basically telling me thank you very much, but go to hell."

This Partial BossHole succeeded in snatching defeat from the jaws of victory. He turned a moment of pride and satisfaction into unbelievable, bitter disappointment. I had put in a tremendous amount of extra effort and enthusiasm into this project. The tradeshow was a huge success by any objective measure. It positively impacted every single store in the chain, and then my boss flushed that all away because he couldn't say, "Good job. Take some time and go kick it. You've earned it." So what did that communicate to me as an employee? That my effort, my time commitment and everything I've done was basically not valued by the organization, as represented by that BossHole attitude. Mind you, he was not a Complete BossHole. For the most part he was a nice person and a gentleman. But he had a knack for doing one or two stupid things a week that would undermine all of his good work.

I think there are three traits that are critical to the success of any good team. Number one, **engagement**, are they actively, willfully, enthusiastically doing the things they need to do, or are they just going through the motions? Are they putting in their hours? Are they just complying with the letter of the law but not the spirit of what was intended?

Engagement is a crucial part of the success of an organization, and the Gallup organization, through their Human Sigma project, strongly suggests through their research that businesses with engaged employees create engaged customers and have 30 to 40% increased profitability. Clearly, employee engagement and customer engagement are key drivers of success. You want to encourage engagement, not discourage it. Refusing to acknowledge a Herculean engaged effort on the fall season tradeshow with a little paid time off made me feel like the boss did not recognize my effort and did not appreciate the value of what I did. And it definitely affected my decision to start looking for a different opportunity.

The second trait to focus on is a concept that I do not know what else to call, so I'm calling it "**how to win awareness**." (HTWA) My brother Tom, who is a baseball coach, explained this to me. Certain players may have a little less physical skill, a little less speed, a little less strength. They don't run as fast, they don't throw as hard, they don't jump as high, but when the game is on the line, they know how to do that little thing that helps the team win. It oftentimes does not show up in the statistics of the game. With a runner on second, and no outs, the batter comes up and intentionally rolls the ball to the second baseman to move the runner from second to third. With one out, the runner can be driven in with a sacrifice fly or with a chopper. The batter gets no credit for this action in the line score because it doesn't count as a hit, but it's a productive out. So there are certain players that know how to position themselves, how to dive when they need to dive, how to throw behind the runner, how to hit behind the runner, how to do the little things that help the team win.

In business, that happens every day. There are employees who know how to smooth over a customer problem, how to recognize when something is not working and jump in and fix it. These are things that are not in the manual, or in your policies and procedures. It's just that there are certain people who simply know how to get it done. Maybe they aren't as fast and maybe they aren't as smart or maybe they aren't as glamorous as some other employees, but when you look at who's in there fixing and solving the problems and moving your team forward, you'll notice that it's always the same people. There are some people who are great at tooting their own horns and pushing their own agenda (Underground BossHoles), but they just don't perform when you need them to, or worse yet, they actually get in the way of success.

The third trait that a Great Boss needs to pay attention to and understand is **role identification.** Does each person on your team perform the role they were given? Sometimes it's not the role he wants, and sometimes it's not the role he would prefer, or even in his mind be best at, but does he take on his role and perform his role as the team needs him to do it?

Suppose you want to be the starting left fielder, but you're not. If you're not going to be the starting left fielder and get four at-bats a game, what can you do to help this team? If you're pouting about not being the starting left fielder and you're not putting your work in, what is the chance you will be ready when your team needs you? If you're not intensely watching the game from the bench, what is the chance you will be seeing something that could help your teammates succeed? If you are upset because you're not the starting left fielder and your behavior manifests as giving anything less than your best effort, then you are in fact hurting the team. You're showing your weakness and your pettiness and your selfishness instead of doing whatever you can within your role to help your team succeed. So what would a good teammate do if he wanted to be the starting left fielder but he didn't get the opportunity? What he should do is say, "I want to be able to help position and talk to the starting left fielder and help him understand who's coming up and remind him of the hitter's tendencies. I am going to do anything I can to help the guy on the field perform better. Then I have to be ready to go in when the team needs me. I have to keep myself in top shape. I have to prepare like I was the starter, but also prepare like I am the secondary person who has a different role."

Part of being a good teammate and helping develop good team chemistry is to play the role of the spot you're in and do it to the best of your abilities. A Great Boss understands the three traits that drive the success of the team: engagement, how to win awareness, and role identification and commitment. BossHoles cause employees to disengage, reward the wrong people, and allow unproductive behavior to become the norm. I believe good leaders must be good people. They must possess the attributes they expect from their employees and not display the negative attributes they don't want in their employees. Good leaders must understand these key drivers of success, but should also be able to critically evaluate the impact of their actions on the team. No leader is perfect. Occasionally they will say or do something counterproductive. The only way to avoid screwing up is to never try to do anything innovative. Of course, the unintended consequences of never trying anything new are an unproductive team.

The penultimate performance trait for a Great Boss is the ability to adjust your tone as necessary. The tone of your leadership is your attitude, your demeanor, how loud you are, how vocal you are, how injected you are into the daily activity. You must understand that any noise or any sound or any pattern that becomes consistent, recognizable and repetitive gets tuned out. If you go to bed with a ballgame playing on the radio, it eventually fades into the background and you fall asleep. If you're sound asleep, and the radio hasn't been on and all of a sudden it starts blaring a homerun call in the seventh-inning, it's going to jolt you out of your sleep.

You're going to wake up and say, "Wait a minute. What was that?"

The leader's tone of voice needs to be adjusted to continually snap your team to attention, to bring them into focus when they need it, to encourage their success and move them forward to where they want to be. It can be used to recognize when the energy and enthusiasm of the group has waned, so that you can provide that impetus to recapture the positive energy you need to succeed. All these things are much easier to define than they are to accomplish. So what is it that leaders need to do in order to pay attention to these things, and to know what to do about it? A quality leader is going to generate their impact based on three things.

First, **creating the climate** that frees your talent, your team, to do the things they are capable of doing. It's not your job to practice hitting, throwing, blocking, tackling, etc. It's your job to create the climate where the talent wants to do that and puts in all the time and energy necessary. The difference between a team engaged and a team going through the motions is that the engaged team is motivated internally to succeed. They identify with and buy into the goals and values of the team. They enjoy the process of improving and working hard in order to meet those goals. Other teams who are only driven by rewards and punishment will follow the rules and will do what they're told, but they won't put in that extra dimension of energy and enthusiasm, and it shows up in their performance. As a leader your primary focus is creating the climate that allows the talent to run free.

Second, you need to be able to **identify the abilities** that the person often doesn't even know they have. It is easy when scouting baseball teams for people to recognize the player that can run fast, throw hard, hit for power, hit for average, and is a great base runner. Everybody sees that person. Great players like Willie Mays, Mickey Mantle, Hank Aaron and Mike Trout did everything well when they were very young. It's much harder to identify which of the late round draft picks is going to blossom into a superstar because his talents are not so obvious. Most players are not going to have readily identifiable superstar traits. The typical player doesn't exude power, speed, energy and enthusiasm. When you land a superstar, great, take advantage of it. However, in most cases you have to look through the mix of player attributes and identify talents that the player doesn't even know they possess. Great Bosses bring these hidden talents out in their people. When you do that, your team will grow, will improve, your players will want to be there, and you can help them become better than they could've been before they met you. The difference between going out and hiring the best players from other teams and building your own is that there are only a few teams that can afford to go out and hire the best players after they've already proven themselves.

There may be a few teams like the Dodgers, Yankees - maybe Boston Red Sox that can go out and just buy players. Most other teams have to develop their own players, have to recognize their abilities, have to foster their skills, have to teach them how to bring those skills out in the game, and have to let them nurture and develop. These Oakland Athletic type teams are the kinds of teams that can compete even though they don't have the big money to spend. And despite the nonsense our mainstream media continually proselytizes as fact, money is not the key motivator for success. Paying people more does not make them play better. Not in sports and not in business. Money is a de-motivator. Not paying people what they are worth will cause them to dis-engage and seek work elsewhere. But people driven to excel are motivated by the desire to win not the money. Since you will rarely, if ever, have the luxury of buying the best from somebody else's team, you should learn to develop your own superstars.

And the third element of success for a leader comes after you have created a climate that frees the players to play up to their full potential. Once you have identified those key abilities in people that maybe they didn't even know they had, you need to consistently **put people in a position to succeed.** BossHoles want to get rid of everyone who fails. They go around threatening employees with termination for every transgression real and imagined. They create a stressful, miserable and destructive fixed-mindset environment. Great Bosses nurture the environment to bring out the best in their people. They create safe, enjoyable and growth mindset environments by building patterns of success through praising good work and offering constructive feedback on how to improve when failure or setbacks happen.

If a teammate is practicing a skill, and learns to build on that skill, and gets a little better at it each time she tries it, her technique is improving. She will be more likely to see that success manifest in performance. A Great Boss builds good habits in people and teaches them the techniques they need at the level needed to succeed. The team will be much more likely to succeed when the skill levels of the team are constantly improving. There are plenty of people with physical talent who lack the mental skills or the integrity or the character to do the job, and so once again, it's your responsibility to bring the best out of people.

## WARNING BOSSHOLE ALERT!

BossHoles will always try to steal other team's top talent. They are so bad at developing skills in their own organization that they can only compete by finding talent that already knows what to do. The only way to prevent BossHoles from stealing your best talent is to create a work environment that no one wants to leave. Great Bosses discover what people do well and put them in the position to succeed. BossHoles do just the opposite. They put people in the wrong place. They try to have them succeed at skills that they are not actually good at, and they destroy the morale and the quality of play.

Let me give you an example, from one of my softball teams. We had a young lady who was an extremely talented athlete. She had a strong arm, was a power hitter and had tremendous athletic ability. She was more athletic than 95% of the players out there, but in this case, her mother especially wanted her to be a pitcher. In order to be a quality pitcher in fast pitch softball, a top-notch player should dedicate 15-20 hours a week to practicing pitching. This would include time getting specialized coaching and working on their mechanics so that they can put the ball where it needs to be put.

During our 16 and under year, it was obvious that this young lady was not putting her time in on pitching.

When she was on the pitching mound she did not look confident. She would not throw hard. She would nibble and fiddle and just wouldn't attack the game. On the days when she wasn't pitching, she was a strong outfielder. She played with tremendous enthusiasm, high-energy, hit phenomenally well and was a naturally outgoing character with exuberant braggadocio.

When it came time to select our final pitching rotation, it became obvious that she was not going to win a spot in it. However, she had a tremendous ability to help our team as an outfielder. When we approached her and said, "Look, we tried several times to get you to put more time in on the pitching and you're not doing it, and you don't seem to enjoy it when you are doing it, so that's perfectly fine. If you don't want to, we don't need you to be that pitcher, but we think you can be a dominant player as an outfielder. We would love you to just go full time to the outfield."

Well, the mom was not happy with that and moved her to a different team, which was her prerogative as a parent, but she never pitched again. The other team put her in the outfield, and she went on to play her college career as an outfielder. Technically, I was right. It didn't help my individual team win any games, but I think that in the overall scheme of things, it was the right choice for this young lady.

Here is the challenge you face as a leader: Do I acquiesce to this parent's desire for her daughter to be a pitcher just so I can keep her on my team? Or do I set the standard of behavior I expect and then act in alignment with my stated goals? Sometimes doing the right thing bites you in the arse. But every time you compromise your values, you weaken your team. In the work environment, it is just as important to place your people in the role for which they are best suited. And just like with this young pitcher, you can't control how other people will react to the decisions you make. You can only control your actions. You either behave according to your mission, vision and values, or you don't.

When you serve the public, you don't always know what customers are going to demand. You don't know for what they're going to ask. There are certain spots in your workflow that you have to have somebody who can make decisions, who can solve problems before they start, who can head things off, who can make sure you accomplish your goals.

Let me give you an example of this. So much of a prescription business now is an insurance billing business. If a patient comes up to the counter and hands in her prescription, and the person takes her name and phone number and puts it in a queue to be filled, it could take 25-30 minutes to work its way through the queue. Then, if the drug is not covered by the insurance when it's entered into the computer, there will be a rejection notice from the insurance. The pharmacy has to go back to the customer and say, "Do you want to pay cash or do you want us to try to call the doctor and have the drug switched to something that is covered by your insurance?" That switching process could then take an hour or two, depending on if the doctor's available, if the patient stayed in the store, those kinds of things. At the end of the day, if you've had to do that 15 or 20 times, you've got 15 or 20 frustrated customers who didn't get what they wanted in the time frame they wanted it. Moreover, you created extra work by having to handle the prescription multiple times. The prescription has to be stopped, has to be special handled, has to go back to the beginning, the doctor has to be called, and the customer has to be inconvenienced.

But what happens if you have an employee at the intake counter who can look at the insurance card and look at the drug that is prescribed and say, "I know this is not covered by this plan so here's what I want you to do. I need you decide if this is something that you need and you'd want to pay for it without insurance, or do you want us to call the doctor and ask for it to be switched to whatever's covered by your insurance?"

If that conversation gets handled right at the intake counter and that customer knows right away that there will be a delay, then she can use her time wisely and go do something else. She's not going to wait for hours while you wait for the doctor's office to respond. The result of that is that the customer's happier, she knows what's going on, she's not just hanging around without information, and it improves dramatically the number of times you have to stop and start and slow down the workflow.

That intake position, in my opinion, should be filled by somebody with experience, somebody who has decision-making skills, somebody who cares enough and is engaged enough to pay attention, to learn what the drugs are, and to learn what's covered by each insurance company. It's something that not everybody can do. Putting the wrong person in that position could destroy your workflow and the productivity of the entire team. Putting the right person in that position makes everything smooth and makes the entire organization work better. Great Bosses think about what really needs to be done at each point of the workflow, and match employee skill sets to jobs in order to enhance group performance. BossHoles put people in the wrong places.

My typical complaint with the chain drugstore industry is they take their newest, least-trained, least-experienced person and they put them on the cash register or at the front of the pharmacy. They take their most experienced, most trained persons, typically the pharmacist or tenured technician, and have them in the back doing the filing. By default, all the customer contact and most of the conversation is with the least experienced, least trained person in the building. That is a recipe for disaster. One of the reasons why independent pharmacies continue to thrive is because they intimately recognize the difference and put the right people where they belong. A critical leadership skill, therefore, is awareness. Awareness of the true skills of your players, awareness of the ways to create an environment that fosters the correct behavior and awareness of the attributes that are fundamental elements of success.

Great Bosses command when their team needs it but avoid micromanaging. They put players where they need to be. They identify and recognize the skills of individual people and nurture and bring out the skills that need to be developed within the team. BossHoles take a solid power hitter and turn her into a weak singles hitter. They take somebody with tremendous speed and agility and put them in a position where they can't use their speed to its full advantage. Great Bosses not only put people in the right position they fine tune performance with consistent training regarding the right way to do the job.

A huge distinction between a Great Boss and a BossHole is the manner in which behavior is corrected. Great Bosses consistently correct faulty behavior as soon as it happens. Bad behavior ignored becomes bad habits. BossHoles either overact to performance stumbles or ignore bad employee behavior. Ignoring poor performance telegraphs to everyone else that it's okay to be a bad employee. Overreacting to poor performances destroys team cohesion. Recognizing and rewarding the right behavior will align your work team and their motivation with the goals, objectives and values of your organization.

One critical mistake a lot of bosses make is modeling the wrong behavior. If you own a store and want to drink a soda, many owners go out and grab a soda and drink it. Employees watching the boss go take a soda and drink it or take a candy bar and eat it without paying for it will say, "Okay, I guess it's okay to take a soda or eat a candy bar without paying for it." Now imagine the different mindset being modeled if every time you go out and get a candy bar or a bag of peanuts or a soda, you make a big show of waiting behind the customers, waiting your turn to pay and paying with cash. You've then modeled a couple of things: Employee snack purchases don't butt cash paying customers out of line and paying for your purchases is hugely important if even the boss who actually owns the entire inventory pays for his or her purchases. So be careful what behaviors you model, and be careful which behaviors you encourage and discourage.

Another classic example in the drugstore business is that there are certain customers that everybody wants to just get rid of. They're annoying, they're whiny, and they're complainers. They've always got a beef about something. As the boss, if you overhear an employee arguing with that kind of customer or complaining about that kind of customer, what do you do? One possible thing you could do is nothing, in which case you have tacitly communicated to your employees that it's okay to argue, complain and whine about customers. Another potential way to deal with it, and what I think you might find to be more useful, would be to not allow arguing and complaining by interjecting yourself in the conversation immediately and saying, "That's not acceptable." If your employee argues that the customer was wrong, you should state that it is quite possible the customer is wrong however that does not give you the right to argue with a customer. It might sound something like this: "That is not your job. Your job as an employee of this company is to make sure every customer wants to come back and spend his hard-earned money with us. Arguing and fussing and being rude do not make that person want to come back here. Now you may think that person doesn't have the right to be rude or to be demanding, and that is your prerogative, but it is not your prerogative to show that to him or to other customers. Because every time you're fighting with a customer, every other customer in the store is seeing that. They don't know the history of this person and that he's a constant whiner. They don't know that. All they know is they saw you being rude to a customer."

Now look at an alternative example. Imagine if a person is being rude, and obnoxious, and you handle them with care and skill and get that person to calm down. Then very carefully you get them to understand what it is you can and cannot do. You communicate a sincere willingness to help them. In this scenario, you've communicated to every customer in the store that you are really good at customer service.

The first time you allow your employees to get rude, mean or argumentative, you've lost control. My view as an independent business owner is that no one has the right to chase off a customer other than you. And owners should reserve this right for very infrequent usage. Because as soon as you model chasing customers off, you have tacitly given permission for your employees to do the same. When there is somebody that you do need to eject, you do it behind closed doors and professionally, and you remind your employees that nobody has the right to send customers and their potential sales revenue out of the building. Now if a customer is making threats, is out of line, is about to do something illegal, it's your responsibility to stand up for your employees and to take that head on. You can't allow your employees to feel threatened or under attack, but you also can't grant them the authority to start chasing people off. They will use it at a much faster rate than you will. The net effect of that is your business will not grow. No employee has the right to give away your customers. A Great Boss will create an environment such that rewards people for turning the grouchy customer into a loyal customer.

One of the real secrets to success of a small business is using a customer complaint or problem as the perfect opportunity to cement your customer service relationship. People understand that there could be problems. People understand that there might be mistakes made. People understand that things aren't always going to go well. If you handle that situation correctly, problems become a catalyst for converting grouchy people into long-term, engaged customers.

In the world of prescription pharmacy, one of the scariest and most upsetting things that can ever happen is when a customer comes to the counter and says there's been a prescription error. "You filled my prescription incorrectly." This does not happen very often, but when it does the natural reaction for a lot of pharmacists is to get defensive. If a customer senses that you're trying to hide anything from them or that you don't care enough to take them seriously or that you are more concerned with saving your butt than making sure that they are okay, then that error could easily become a nightmare for the pharmacy.

Not only will that error be a problem for the customer, but it's going to become a real big problem for you. An angry person who is treated poorly is now twice as angry and will go out and tell 8-10 people not to come to your store, because you messed up. Contrast that again with a different approach. Imagine a customer comes in and says, "Hey, I think there's been a prescription error made. I think I got the wrong medicine." If the pharmacist looks the customer in the eye and says, "Oh my gosh, are you okay? Is there anything that we need to do to make sure that you are okay? Do you need me to take you over to Dr. Smith here and get checked out? Because I don't know what happened yet and I want to look into that, but my first thing is to make sure you're okay."

Once we know the answer to that, let's go look into it. "Show me what you have, show me what you think was wrong, and then I'll dig into it and find out what happened." So rather than being defensive, rather than being evasive, you step right in with, "Are you okay? Is there anything I can do to alleviate your discomfort?" Then you've defused 99% of the anger.

So let's get back to what leadership is all about. Leadership is about having answers to these key questions. Are you aware of the real performance issues? Are you rewarding your people on the right metric? Are your people engaged? Do they solve problems or do they create them? Do they know how to win? Are your customers engaged and are they recommending you to their friends? Are you putting people in the right roles to help your team? Are your people where they can do you the most good? Are you able to adjust the tone as needed to keep your team focused and energetic? Are your people excited to come to work and do they get along with each other? Do you know how to create the climate to free your talent, to identify the abilities of your people, and to put people in a position to succeed? Do they work for you because they want to or because they need a job? Great Bosses can answer these questions correctly. BossHoles wonder why anyone would ask these dumb questions. Great Bosses create good businesses. BossHoles just act like BossHoles until there is no business left to ruin.

# Chapter 7: Creating a Value Strategy

**"The man who will use his skill and constructive imagination to see how much he can give for a dollar, instead of how little he can give for a dollar, is bound to succeed." Henry Ford**

A critical step in developing a good business is creating a sound value strategy. You can be the best boss in the world but if your business strategy doesn't resonate with the market you will not succeed. Another way of saying this using the coaching metaphor is how do you want to play the game? What style of play do you want to be known for? Are you going to be a three-run home run guy? Are you going to be a speed and take the extra base guy? How are you going to design your team to be successful? You can increase your likelihood of being a successful coach if you understand the key ingredients of producing a successful result.

In baseball, the goal is to score more runs than the other team. It doesn't matter if your team ERA, team batting average, or average runs scored per game is above or below the league average. The only real metric that counts in the grand scheme of things is how many games did you win? You get into the playoffs based on how many games you've won.

When it comes to understanding how to build and craft a team in order to win games, there are two interesting subplots. Number one is that there are certain metrics and statistics that, over the long haul, predict the ability to win more often than not. The science of baseball analysis is called sabremetrics, invented by a fellow named Bill James. The book *Money Ball* chronicled how Billy Beane and the Oakland Athletics used these techniques to produce playoff caliber teams. Theo Epstein and the Red Sox won two world championships using these new metrics to identify players and craft a roster capable of winning. The essence of the sabremetric approach to baseball is to identify the best statistical predictors and use those as a guide for constructing a team and a line-up card for each game.

However, in any short five-game or seven-game stretch, the odds don't necessarily play out in favor of the long-term predictors. Individual performance drives the success of any team in a short series. So given those two competing standards –a set of strategies that lead to wins over the long haul, and the individual performance required to win any given game, how will you choose to lead? There are certain traits and characteristics that seem to produce wins more often. So understanding the key drivers of what helps you win is an important thing to know as a coach. It's also important to know as a Great Boss. There are certain things Great Bosses do that tend to lead to more successful outcomes, and there are certain risks you take that tend to not be worth the risk.

The baseball axiom is that pitching and defense win championships, but great defensive teams with great pitching still have to score runs in order to win. In business, the win is making the sale, growing the business, dominating the market share or making your competition irrelevant. Regardless of the goal, successful businesses need to be able to do three things well to consistently develop and compete in the marketplace.

1.  **Identify** a pain in the marketplace. What do customers say is missing? What do they want and would gladly pay for if somebody would just give it to them? Identifying this pain in the marketplace allows you to craft a strategy to fulfill that need, which will energize your growth and catapult you into a market share position.

2.  **Develop** a solution to remedy that pain, to ease that pain, or to fill that market void. There are lots of ways you can craft a solution for the marketplace. However, if you don't understand what the true drivers of purchase behavior are, no strategy is likely to succeed. Thus, understanding what really drives purchase behavior or the decision to buy is also critical.

3.  **Make an offer** to your target market. The one piece of the puzzle that many people forget is that you have to put your offer in front of the customer. You have to offer to provide the solution that people want to have. If you never make an offer you will rarely get paid.

Those three challenges - identifying a market, developing a solution and offering to perform - require a Great Boss to design a business plan that will adhere to these three standards. Businesses that resonate with the marketplace and grow quickly follow this simple process. Of course, there are numerous other challenges along the way. You need to be able to scale and grow the business. You want to protect your idea from theft, and your business model has to earn a profit. However, the essential driver of a successful strategy is understanding why people buy what they buy. Why do they not buy what they don't buy? What would make them buy what you offer instead of what somebody else is offering? Fail to understand this, and your chances of success plummet.

I believe that to make this as simple as possible and as actionable as possible, there are really only three things you need to know about what drives people to make a purchase, use your service, or select what you have to offer instead of what your competition offers. I published an article in the journal, *Research in Social and Administrative Pharmacy* titled, "The Value Prescription: Relative Value Theorem as a Call to Action," in the summer of 2011, describing this process as the Relative Value Theorem. These three elements are as follows:

The first and most recognizable element, of course, is the price. What does it cost? But be careful not to equate this with strictly the dollars and cents. Let me explain what I mean. If two items are identical and they're both offered at the same price – let's say that price is $29.95 - that does not mean that those two items cost the same. Because included in the price/cost calculation for this service is not just the dollars and cents I have to part with, but the energy I have to expend, the time I have to put into it, the emotional drain it costs me to buy from you. All of the costs in time, energy, enthusiasm, money and effort go into the component that I'm describing as price.

In other words, what it costs me to buy your product is not only the dollars that come out of my bank account. It is also the time it takes me to go to your store to pick it up, the gasoline it costs me to drive over there, the aggravation I have to experience waiting in line at your business, and the annoyance I get when it's not ready yet and I have to come back multiple times. The opportunity cost of what I could've been doing with that time rather than sitting around waiting in your stores is also part of the price. Multiple factors go into the price of your service. Understanding that price is one element critical to your development of a solution to ease a pain in the marketplace. How can you craft an offering that your targeted customer will calculate as being lower-cost? There are different ways to accomplish this task.

The most obvious is the Walmart Strategy, where it costs them less dollars out of their bank account. That's the traditional discounting approach. Essentially, Walmart says to their targeted consumer, "We're going to offer everything at the lowest out of pocket cost, and therefore, you know when you go to Walmart that you're going to get a lower price." That's their marketing strategy. It's been very effective for them.

But I would argue that this is probably not the right strategy for a locally owned independent business, primarily because it's very difficult to pull off. There's only one way you can be the low-cost leader, and that's to sell everything at the lowest price. In order to be able to sell everything at the lowest possible price, you would need to wring all non-essential costs out of your business model. To buy everything at a better cost, to be able to sell it at a lower price, requires leverage with suppliers. To operate at the lowest operating costs requires high sales volume and inexpensive labor and rent. Those are not things that the typical small business can pull off. Pursuing a low price strategy may actually be counterproductive. If you call yourself the low price leader and a customer checks only to find out that you are more expensive, you will have driven a wedge of mistrust into your relationship. Customers will begin to doubt you. They won't trust you. They won't come back. Consider this: if every competitor had this same strategy in a competitive marketplace, only one company could possibly be telling the truth. The rest would essentially be lying to their customers. The Walmart strategy is available, it is just very difficult to execute. Fortunately, there are other strategies available to small businesses.

A small local business can make the argument that it costs the consumer less time and energy, gasoline or effort to shop at the local option rather than drive the extra ten miles to go to the big-box store. That is another way to influence the price element of the Relative Value Theorem. If you apply your knowledge of all the elements that factor in to the cost, other than just the dollars spent, several other options become clear. Other questions a business can pose to identify the true cost drivers for their product or service are:

How many times do you have to go back to the store to get your order completed? How long do you have to wait in my store versus their store? How easy is it for you to get in and out of the store? (This is hugely important for people with limited mobility). Do you feel welcomed and appreciated? Is the business process user friendly and stress free? If the small local operator saves the customer effort or money in another area by offering extra services that save money, they can promote this price advantage. Eventually the customer evaluates your price offering as the sum of dollars that comes out of her bank account and the combined other costs to her in time, energy, aggravation and effort. Deciding how to position your product or solution in the marketplace clearly requires a sound pricing strategy using this complete definition of price.

Now, what happens if the only marketing strategy you do have is price? Well, the easiest thing for a lousy competitor to do to attract new business is to lower their price. That competitor may be able to lower that price to a level that is unprofitable for you. Bad companies mistakenly believe that they can lower prices below profitability to attract customers, and then eventually raise the price up to where they'll be profitable. In any marketplace, there's always some competitor that tries to offer a product at a lower price as their strategy to increase sales. However, it's a very difficult strategy to pull off and stay profitable over the long haul, unless you continually improve efficiency. To say you are, in fact, going to be the low price leader all the time on all items is risky. As soon as you're not, you will lose the customer's trust.

Apparently, Walmart can't even make the Walmart strategy work on all product categories. There is too much competition from too many different distribution channels. It is significant that Walmart changed their slogan from "Always the Low Price Leader" to "Always Low Prices" in 1988, and then in 2007 changed their slogan again to "Save Money, Live Better."

Once an item sells strictly based on its price, whoever has the lowest price gets the sale, and whoever doesn't have the lowest price doesn't get the sale. That item then becomes a commodity. When you look at a business strategy for an individual business owner or an individual professional, becoming a commodity is not going to be a long-term successful strategy. Someone else will always offer it cheaper.

So while price is important, it's clearly not the only thing that drives business. If it were, then only the business with the absolute lowest price would stay in business. Everybody else would do zero sales. I've never found any market where that's true. There's clearly something else also at work here, because even though one company sells a set of four tires for $300 and another sells that identical set for $350, the company charging the higher price is still doing some business. So what is that other element besides just how many dollars it costs me, what the price is and what it costs me in time, energy and aggravation to drive over there?

The second element is service. What else do I get with the product in addition to the product itself? What side benefits do I get with a purchase from you in addition to just purchasing the product? Well, what exactly does this term "service" mean? The service component of an offering is everything that comes with the product over and above the product itself. In other words, if I'm offering to fill your prescription for a $10 co-pay, the $10 co-pay is the price, and you're getting a filled prescription for that. The other things that you might get from me, such as personalized service, free home delivery, expert consultation, a friendly face, a neighborly atmosphere in the store, those are things that are not exactly part of the product. They're additional add-on features, benefits, or services provided by my way of selling you this product.

The component of service adds a new layer of complexity to the purchase decision. What we'll see is people might say, "Well it's cheaper to go over there. That guy sells it for $2.00 cheaper, but when I come in here, they know my name, it's always ready, they give me great advice and they help me pick out my over-the-counter medications that go along with the prescription. These extra services are worth something to me. Therefore, even though the price is a little bit cheaper somewhere else, I'm going to patronize this particular pharmacy because I like what else they have to offer."

That is the essence of a service offering that you have to design as a Great Boss and as a marketer. You have to observe the marketplace and be aware of current trends. You have to know what's going on. You have to know what people are charging for things. You have to know how they conduct their business and how they present their offering to the public. Are they a high-service, high-touch business? Are they a low-cost leader, low-service business? These are all things that you have to understand about your competition to know where to position your business to attract the level of market and level of customers that you want. To understand how to create value for a customer, you clearly have to comprehend the pricing component and understand the competitive service offerings.

You must know the additional services, additional benefits, and all of the things that come with the sale other than just the original product. Some competitors may offer price matching, price guarantees, product warranties, buyer education or additional consultation as add-on services to their product offering. Are price and service all that goes through people's heads when they decide to buy something? If it was strictly price and service, then the person with the lowest price and the best service, theoretically, should have all the sales. What we see in the real marketplace is different. There is not one business that just dominates every single sale within a marketplace. So what is this other element that goes into deciding why we buy something? I will use an example of a car purchase here to make my point.

When I was a starving student, didn't have any money, living on student loans trying to get my degree, I bought a 1963 Chevy Impala for $150. It was the lowest priced thing I could get. It ran and that was about all that I was concerned with. I needed something to get from point A to point B. As I progressed in my career, got a job and started making a decent living, that car was no longer acceptable as a vehicle for my needs.

It still drove. It could still get from point A to point B, but it was no longer something that I wanted to have. I wanted something a little sportier, a little fancier. When I went back to my reunion with all my high school buddies, I didn't want to be driving a '63 Impala. I wanted to be driving a new car. Why? Because I wanted to show some outward sign that I was doing okay, and rolling up in a '63 Impala with a dented fender wouldn't have projected the image that I was looking to project - that I was now fairly successful. So obviously, the price was cheaper for a '63 Impala than for a 1980 BMW 320I. The Impala required no down payment and no monthly payments. It didn't have high insurance. It didn't have high repair bills or a lot of the baggage that came with the new vehicle. It was certainly more expensive to drive a brand new 1980 BMW than a paid for '63 Impala.

The other element that made the difference was how the purchase made me feel. Did it allow me to project the image that I wanted to project? Did this purchase satisfy a need that has nothing to do with the transaction, but everything to do with how I perceived myself as a consumer, businessman, family person and leader? As I progressed through my career, having a nice car was more important than having a cheap car. Not everybody would make that same decision, but the reality is that the third element, perceived value, does factor in to the purchase equation. In addition to the price and service, people do indeed consider the perceived value of the purchase.

The third element that helps people decide what to buy is perceived value. How does it make me feel? How badly do I want it? How much do I wish to own that vehicle? How much does it project the image I want to project?

A buyer may wish to buy a nice dress. She may be able to find a nice dress at either Nordstrom's or Target, but she might not shop for that dress at Target because she wants to be able to tell her friends she bought the dress at Nordstrom's. One element of the purchase decision will always be the perceived value of the purchase. The perceived value is going to vary by individual. If she can't afford to buy it anywhere else, then even though she would really like to buy it from Nordstrom's, she still may not do it. She might love to be dressed in all Nordstrom's clothes, but if she doesn't have enough money in her budget, she has to seek less expensive options. Those are not good/bad or a right/wrong decisions. What they are is the real world intervening with your perceptions and desires.

So when you're crafting and developing a solution to the marketplace, the first thing you have to understand is that no single offer is going to appeal to everybody. Secondly, you need to understand that even though buyers may want what you have to offer, they may not be able to afford it right now. One of the biggest mistakes novice business owners make is to overestimate the market response to their offer. They become disappointed when they don't get rich overnight. They build their fixed expenses faster than the potential revenue that can support these expenses, but please, please don't get your spending ahead of your sales.

There's only one way that you know how the market is going to respond to your offer and whether or not that offer is going to be successful: by putting the offer out there. You may think you've come up with the best price, and you may think you've crafted the best service and benefits around your product. But the marketplace may react entirely different, because you misread the perceived value of this.

Let me give you an example: Our drugstore in Sun City, California serviced a town of about 15,000 people, mostly senior citizens, many of whom required incontinence supplies to be an aide to their daily living. At the time, a pack of 18 adult diapers cost $12.99, and somebody who needs them might go through 2-3 diapers a day. For people living on a fixed income, this was a significant expense. I looked out to the marketplace and saw a large block of people that needed the product. I saw some of the embarrassment they felt when they had to go into the store and buy these products. I saw that diapers were fairly expensive at $13 for 18 for a 5-6 day supply; so $13 for 5 days means every month they're spending $78 to buy diapers.

My rational brain said that if I could figure out a way to lower the cost and to make it easier to purchase those diapers that would be a wonderful addition to the marketplace and would be successful. I spent quite a bit of time finding a resource that could maximize efficiencies in the purchase. Instead of having one bag of 18, I could get a box of 72 diapers for a substantially lower cost per diaper. I negotiated a low enough cost from the distributor to allow me not just to buy the product cheaper, but to actually ship and deliver the product directly to someone's home. My guess was that if they didn't have to go out and make that embarrassing purchase, and if I could ship the product at a lower price than they could buy off the shelf, that I would corner the market on adult diapers.

I reviewed competitive prices and my product was cheaper. I looked at the quality of the product, and my product was just as good. I looked at the extra benefits of home delivery. Some of these folks weren't driving any longer. They didn't drive, so they had to walk over to the store. I thought it would be an advantage not having to lug back these big bags of diapers.

So what happened? Well, I put this offering out to the marketplace, I promoted it for several months, and basically had 3-4 people that signed up and took advantage of it. After investing $4,000-5,000 in advertising and getting only several hundred dollars in sales as a return, I started thinking, "What's gone wrong?" I started talking to customers and saying, "How come you don't think this is a good deal?" And the response surprised me. They said, "I can't afford to spend $70 for a box of diapers. I can spend $13 every five days, but I don't have enough to spend $70 once per month to get the same amount of diapers." So it was a cash flow problem. If I had asked my customers before launching, I would've known about this hurdle before I wasted all the time and energy building the product and devoting time and energy to the concept.

In reality, my pricing was better, the service offering of home delivery was better. But the perceived value of saving $8 every month to get home delivery was not. The customer's thinking was, "I can't afford to give up the extra cash out of my bank account. It's not worth the risk to me, because I might have something that comes up that I need to spend that money on." It was really a cash flow item. I learned very clearly that it's not just price, service and benefits; it also includes the filter of the individual consumer's perceived value. And that perceived value is not limited to merely whether or not I want it. It's going to be whether I can afford to do it. The individual perceived value calculation analyzes how this offer compares to all the other potential uses of my money.

One of the big mistakes I made in the early years, and one of the biggest mistakes a lot of entrepreneurs make, is looking at your product or service offering only in the realm of competing with other similar product offerings. I was looking at adult diapers and comparing it to all other sources of adult diapers. The customers were comparing it to other uses of their money.

When we think we are selling over-the-counter vitamins, the consumer is actually saying, "I've got $30 to spend. I can spend it on vitamins, I can spend it on a movie, I can spend it on going out to dinner, I can spend it on a book, I can spend it on a doctor's visit or I can spend it on ice cream." For them, the value equation is determined by comparing what you're selling to all alternate uses of their time, energy and money. This one single understanding changed my life as a marketer, because I began to understand the real motivations that cause people to buy or not buy. At this point, what you need to internalize is that there are three things that people use to decide whether or not they're going to buy your product or service.

1. What is the **price/cost** in time, money, and energy for me to buy the product?

2. What are the **services** and extra benefits I get from buying the product from choice A versus choice B versus choice C?

3. **How badly do I want** or need this product, and can I afford to use my limited amount of money to buy this product versus all other options I have for spending that money?

The essence of creating value for your customers is learning how to modify your price and service offering to compete in the marketplace of competitive offerings within your target market. In addition, learning how to craft your marketing efforts to enhance the perceived value of the product compared to all other uses of their money is critical. As a business person, the only thing under your direct control is the price and service offering. The perceived value component is internal to the person or organization making the decision to buy. If you want to be effective as a business person, I suggest that you spend a lot more time up front understanding the purchase motivation for your potential customer before you waste time on the price and service. Great Bosses understand how these three elements interact, BossHoles always seem to leave one out of the discussion.

The lucrative opportunities in the marketplace come when you find a pain in the marketplace. This pain represents a demand or unmet need in the marketplace which potential purchasers are begging you to fill. Once you develop a solution to ease that pain, the customers will be primed to buy. Your marketing is much easier and much more successful when customers are standing in line to buy your product before you even open for business. Pre-selling the market builds demand. The last remaining hurdle to success is to simply make the offer to sell.

The novice business person thinks along a linear pathway: develop a product, market the product, and sell the product. The experienced marketer thinks in reverse order. They figure out what people are aching to buy, and then find a way to sell it to them. If you train yourself to think backwards and find out what consumers want to buy first, you can develop a solution to the pain in the market that will appeal to that market segment's internal motivation to buy. Developing a product that meets the needs of a hungry market will greatly improve your chance of success.

A hungry market waiting to pounce on a viable solution will speed the rate at which your offering will be purchased. Marketing that offers a solution to a pre-sold market is virtually guaranteed to succeed. If you have crafted the offer correctly and you've developed a solution that meets the internal motivational needs of the purchaser rather than the procedural needs of your business, you are much more likely to make the sale.

Because most marketers and most business people fail to perform their research correctly at the beginning, there are always opportunities to develop products and services that appeal specifically to people ready to buy the solution. These can be sold without expensive marketing efforts, because the market is already searching for your solution. Your competition will wonder why and how you got the order when they've been trying to sell their solution for years. Answer the internal motivation question first, and then design the solution.

So let me circle back to the issue of how people decide what to buy. The unimaginative business discounts their price as their marketing strategy. A smarter business thinks backwards to identify a hungry market. A key advantage of the backwards development of a product is the market is focused on the solution, not the price. A hungry market understands what the lack of a solution is costing them.

If a customer is spending $1 million a year because they can't resolve a shipping problem, and you can resolve that shipping problem for them by offering a service that removes their main roadblock, what is that service worth to the potential purchaser? It's worth at least $1 million. You may be able to provide that service for something substantially less than that. But when you understand what the real motivation for your buyer is, what the real costs to that business are, then you can offer a solution that either saves them money, earns them more money, or eliminates a big opportunity cost for them. And you can do that in a way where you've now shifted the price discussion from "how do I compare to three other people offering something similar" to "how much money am I going to save you?" So, the net impact of the purchase of your product is a net gain to the customer.

Let me be clear on that. Suppose, in trying to sell your service, you say, "My service costs $500 a month, and I will do XYZ, and from XYZ you're going to get the following benefits." What you're asking the purchaser to do is think about that, calculate where he is going to get the $500 a month and then decide whether or not that $500 a month is going to give him anything in return. Clearly it's good for you since you get $500, but he may not understand or see what that $500 a month is going to get for him. So flip that discussion on its ear. Your purchaser is spending $5,000 a month to do a particular thing. You come in and say, "I know that you're spending $5,000 per month on this. We're going to take all of this headache away from you and we're going to do it for $2,500 a month." What does that purchase cost your purchaser? It costs him an improvement of $2,500 a month, which means he'd be crazy not to buy your solution if it works.

Which of those offers do you think is more likely to be successful? Pay me $500 a month and try to figure out what it's worth for you or to work with me, and I will give you $2,500 a month. The secret to small business success is that you need to be responsive to the needs of your client at a level the big businesses just can't, because nobody's paying attention to it at this granular level.

Where you can succeed and where you're going to thrive as a small business person is by identifying a pain in the marketplace, crafting a solution to ease that pain and then crafting an offer to be put in front of people that is a clear win for them. When you do that, you can be on your way to having a successful business model. Once you understand how value is created, you need to begin crafting a strategy that has a good likelihood of succeeding in creating value in the mind of your targeted consumer. There are a few things that I need to explain further.

When you are the boss of a team, you are required to set the tone for that team. You must decide the style of play you wish to use and for which you want your team to be known. A big part of that strategy style involves aligning your business principles and your core set of beliefs with your business model so that everything that you do resonates with your core values. If you have a great plan to become a power hitting team, but you coach and develop players who run fast and play defense, you're going to find out that you have a mismatch between your daily activities, your daily practicing, your daily coaching and your stated goals with your actual execution of those goals.

For a baseball team to be successful using a team-based strategy of bunting, moving the runner, hitting behind the runners, taking pitches to increase opposing pitcher pitch counts and win in the late innings, by playing solid defense, you need to create the foundation for that plan to succeed. In order to develop that strategy, and to be successful using that strategy, your practice sessions have to practice the skills needed. Your personnel development has to involve attracting the kinds of players that fit your style. Your coaches have to coach your style. Your decisions made in games have to implement that style and you have to be constantly developing and tweaking your actions to fit your style of play. An analogous process is necessary to build a winning business team. If my business is a high-touch, high-service, take care of the individual customer kind of business, then I have to design business systems that make sure that I execute on that promise.

You cannot be the low price leader, eliminate all the extra payroll from your workflow, have just-in-time delivery of product and also say you're going to give the highest level of service. The two do not match; they can't match, because you have to build the team differently. You have to build your workflow differently. You have to build your customer service strategy differently based on your core values. Defining yourself as the low price leader comes with a whole set of continual activities to maintain that value.

Considering yourself a high service, hands-on, meet-every-need-that-you-have kind of service provider means that your system must support that mission. Your people have to be trained to do that. Your policies and your staffing levels have to be higher. You might have to pay people a little more, because you want people that can execute on that every single time, not just every now and then, when they feel like it. So there's an entire style of play strategy that you have to align with. Regardless of which style of play you decide as a business, there are three things that you have to do in order to make sure that you have the internal resources and competencies to pull off your strategy.

First, you must examine the core values that you believe in and build a strategy that resonates with your core values. The reason this is so critical is that, over time, based on the daily activities, based on the practice, based on the game management, a team always assumes the personality and demeanor of its leader. If you are a fun-loving, outgoing, casual, personal, very hands on coach, the team's going to play differently than if you're a restrictive, autocratic, follow the rules, scream and yell kind of coach. If you try to be someone you are not, it never seems to work out well in the long run.

To build a business plan that works you must match the business model with your natural style. You may think that you can change your natural style, but I have never seen it happen. If strategically you want to develop a high touch, high service business, but your basic core values are always to find the lowest cost, cheapest deal available, you will have a problem staying with the high touch strategy over the long haul. If you are someone that believes in cheap, cheap, cheap, it's really hard for you to turn your head around and say, "I have to hire better people. I have to give more hours. I have to put an extra person here, because our lines are getting too long at a certain time of the day."

On the other hand, if you're a person that says, "Regardless of cost, I think we get a payoff by having an excellent customer interface and a real strong customer experience. It may not make dollars and cents today, but it's going to expand my business and increase my referral capacity. I'm going to get more customers over the long haul, because they're going to tell their friends how great we do in customer service," that would resonate with your core better. You can't mix and match without causing a problem.

If you honestly believe that one strategy is better than the other, and you don't have the core values it takes to pull it off, it doesn't mean you can't build a business around it. However, it does mean you need to put someone on the operations management team who has those skills and mindset and will execute this vision and keep it on track.

The second thing that you absolutely have to do is align the style with your strengths. Once you've decided on a strategy, then all your business practices, all your hiring practices, all your training practices, all the discipline of your employees must align with that style, must encourage that style, must reward people that do it well and correct people that do it wrong. If you allow people within your workflow not to do what you want them to do, then by default, you're not going to execute on that promise. You're not going to go out to the marketplace and say "here's what we do" and have customers come in and actually get that experience. If you advertise that you are a high service business, and then customers come in and wait in long lines and get bad service, the customers will be disappointed. They won't trust you. They will leave and find someplace else to spend their money. If you market high service, and they receive great service, they will instantly recognize the difference between you and your low service competition. They will be much more likely to say, "Wow, this is cool" and tell their friends. The challenge is to constantly review your hiring practices, your workflow, your scheduling and your layout to make sure that you're executing on your promise. You need to religiously do everything you can to align your daily actions with your strategy.

And third, you have to select the right people to be on your team. Basically you have to cast your play to include the right actors. You must find people who believe that your strategy is the right way of doing it. You must be able to trust that their core values are aligned with the values and core beliefs of your business. If they are not, you need to determine quickly if they never will be or if they will respond favorably to additional training.

This is a tough call sometimes, but in my opinion, if after two weeks a new employee cannot get aligned with your style of business, they're never going to get aligned. That's when you need to decide who wins the part in your play. If two weeks into rehearsals, the bad actor wants to play Shakespeare with a German accent when you require an English accent, then you've got to find a different actor. That's just the way it goes. Great Bosses ruthlessly protect their core values by quickly getting rid of outliers and by educating those that can improve. BossHoles bring in the wrong people, put them in the wrong jobs, and then blame it on the employee when it doesn't work out.

Interestingly enough, when you allow somebody to stay in your system who doesn't follow the rules you have set, you create a mismatch between what you say you want and what you demonstrate that you allow. When that happens, you have defeated the entire strategy. The people who believed you and bought in say, "Well, he doesn't really mean it." The people that never bought in and don't want to do it say, "So I can get away with whatever I want," and you've just destroyed the capability of your team to deliver on their promise.

Contrast that with "We've hired a new person. We've told them how we want it. We've modeled how we want it. They refused to do it so we removed them." That's one more reminder for everybody on your team that "You see? She believes it, she means it." If you don't do it the way we do it here, then you're free to go do it somewhere else.

Let me give you an example of how your decision making and your vision need to be in alignment. If my vision for a great softball team is one built on speed and on-base percentage I might recruit fast left-handed hitters that can chop the ball on the ground and beat the throw to first base. However, if I have recruited players with that skill then late into a game with the winning run on second base I cannot expect that player to morph in to a power hitter. To expect a player recruited and trained in a certain skill to do something entirely foreign to their ability when the game was on the line would be crazy. As a management strategy, the likelihood of success is very low. There are a few players that have both speed and power, but I'm using the example of somebody that just had the one skill set. The moral of the story is that you don't want to recruit, teach and train a certain way, and then demand that your team do something else, when the game is on the line. That will destroy confidence. That will create a mismatch between what you say you want and what you actually want.

This all left handed hitting team in my example has a structural design flaw that is the responsibility of the leader to fix. The team needs a power hitting pinch hitter to substitute in that late inning scenario. This team needs somebody on the bench who has trained for the role of coming up with two outs and the runner on second base and driving in the run. If you coach by a team-based philosophy and everybody knows their role, buys into that role, understands that role and trains for that role, then you're putting your players in a position to succeed.

If you don't organize your team properly, and don't train people for these roles, and see what you have and what they're capable of, you're going to have a situation that creates failure. When that young lady comes up with the game on the line, and you pull her out to bring somebody else in, she will feel like she's not worthy and you will have destroyed her confidence. She will then disengage and diminish the team effort.

So I am going to repeat myself here because I think it is that important. An essential element of success for your team is, aligning your goals, core values, strategy and practice plans to excel at the way you want to play the game. In addition to selecting the right players, understanding how to coach them, command them, and create the environment where they will thrive is critical. In order to thrive, your goals, strategies, and leadership

111

decisions must be aligned. Any misalignment will cause discord within your team. Great Bosses are adept at keeping the team aligned with their values. BossHoles create confusion.

Once you've decided on your strategy, and which stakeholders you're going to serve, the next step is building a team that has the skills you are likely to need in the full range of situations your team might face. The best way I can explain this is compare once again to a baseball season. There are really several general versions of the game that actually play out over the course of a season. As I mentioned earlier in about a third of the games one team will win in a blowout. In about another third of the games the same team will lose in a blowout. And in the final third of the games the score is competitive and either team could win.

So there are times when you have superior talent and you do everything right and you don't win, and there are times when you have inferior talent, you get lucky and you do win. That's the nature of the game. A good leader will understand that each of those game types requires a different style of in-game management to be successful. You have to make different decisions in each of those games to emerge with a victory.

In order to play all those kinds of games, you have to have a strategy for when you get in those situations. You have to have the right assortment of players on your team, and you need to have trained them for all of those eventualities. Far too often, businesses will come up with a business model and a strategy, and then just assume this is the only thing that's ever going to happen, this is the way it's going to go, and their people don't know what to do when something unusual happens.

But when you look at a business, and let's use a pharmacy for an example, what are the skills, what are the team member attributes a customer service team needs to operate in a high-volume retail pharmacy environment?

- Do you have the people you need so that on those really busy days after a four-day weekend you can efficiently handle that workflow?
- Can you have somebody who normally doesn't do the filling or normally doesn't do the inputting, but when you need them, you can take them away from a different task and move them into the role so that you're not way behind all day long?
- Do you have the customer service people with the right attitude that can handle the pressure on a given day?
- Do you have the filling capacity?
- Do you have the people that can check the labels and do the consultations?
- Do you have all the components you need so that you can handle an overload day where it's twice as busy, because of a four-day weekend or a day when your best technician is out sick?
- Do you have to move people around just to get the job done?
- On a day when there's an audit going on, and you've got the boss tied up doing other

things, do you have people that can cover the boss' normal duties?

These are all different kinds of days that you can have. What do you do on a slow day? When there are no customers are there people that you can divert to other tasks that will help you get ready for inventory or clean off old stock or rearrange displays to improve sales, or whatever it is? You need to be able to say, "What are the elements I need on my team, and when do I deploy them to do what they need to do?" Maybe on a slow day I've got a person who can break out and do some outside marketing by visiting some doctor's offices. Do I have that person who has the personality and understands what we're doing and can go execute my marketing plan?

The reality is life is in a constant state of flux, and the same team can flow between all of these positions depending on injuries, whether they're tired, if there is bad weather, if they have personal issues or off the field issues. You need to be able to mix and match the components to get the right things done on time. This is critical to consistent execution of your strategies. It ensures that when your customers engage with your business, they get the experience you want them to have that aligns with your core values and produces the perceived value in the marketplace that you're trying to develop by your pricing strategy and your service strategy. If you want to be able to execute on that promise, have you dealt with all the contingency plans?

Have you built the capacity into your business to handle vacations, holidays, overload days, and days with few customers? If you haven't, it will cost you at some point, because those days will happen. If you have, you have a better chance of executing on your promise to the customers. If you have great people, but you haven't talked about this, what will happen on a day when things aren't as busy as they normally are? You've got people standing around gabbing instead of doing something productive that's going to help move your business forward.

So at any step of the process as the leader of the business, you need to be able to understand what your core values are, where your strengths are, what you're trying to project to the customer base. You need to understand the strengths and weaknesses of your staff. You need to put them in the place they need to be to be successful. Moreover, you need to be able to look downstream and say, "In order to get this to happen in a couple of months, I have to start doing stuff now that aligns with all of this."

You must know the status of your team. Do I have everybody there? Are they healthy? Are they worn out? Are they underworked? Are they overworked? You must be able to recognize the game you're in – are we in a blowout? Are we in a battle? Are we in the kind of situation where I am going to need to save my bats? And then you have to manage the daily activities to give you the best opportunity to succeed. Now, let me give you an example of how this can work.

You might have a really good pitcher on your softball team, and she's able to pitch as well as any other pitcher in the tournament that you're in. When you start the day fresh, this girl is unbelievable. But what if you get into the loser's bracket and on Saturday you've got to win five games to get to Sunday and the championship round? That same pitcher who is awesome pitching game one is less awesome by game three, and by game five is very beatable. So do you have the right depth on your team? Do you have the right pitching on your team? Do you have the right players in the event that things don't go as you want?

Answering these types of proactive questions is a critical part of leadership. Great Bosses need to honestly assess the limitations of their team well before they get into the critical tournaments and take steps to remedy those limitations. And then when the critical games are underway, the leader needs to recognize the game they are in and make the moves necessary to give her team the best opportunity to win that game.

Let me give you an example. There was a tournament when my team of 11-year olds, was playing up against an older team of mature 12-year olds in a tournament elimination game. If we lost the game, we were out of the tournament. If we won, we continued on. The other team was very powerful and they loved hitting against hard throwing pitchers. Our number one pitcher threw the ball really hard for a girl her age, but our opponents were older, stronger and bigger. In the first inning, they smashed several deep balls, and we were behind 3-0. I'm thinking to myself, "I threw my best pitcher at them, and they smashed it. She cannot throw the ball past these kids. So continuing on this pathway is suicide. If I bring in my next best pitcher, she throws a little bit less hard, but she's going to get lit up too, because this is just the way it is. We're outmatched."

So I did something unusual in that I took my right fielder, who was a lefty and pitched in her recreational ball league, but never pitched on our team, and I told her to come in and pitch. I said, "I understand this is unusual, but I've seen you pitch in practice and I know that you can throw the ball over the plate. What I want you to do is throw it as slow as possible over the plate. I don't want you to try and throw the ball past these girls. What I want you to do is throw slowly, give me a little spin and just do not try to throw the ball hard. Get it over the plate, and let's just see what happens."

For three or four innings we were able to frustrate them, because they couldn't adjust to the ultra-slow speed. They hit a lot of choppers, pop-ups and a lot of weak ground balls. We ended up losing the game, but we stayed in the game, we competed. We had a great time. We did what we needed to do to stay in the game. Late in the game, we actually had the tying run on base and my third baseman hit a double that would have put us in position to tie the game. But she ended up getting thrown out at third base. Some knucklehead in the third-base coaching box, namely myself, got all excited and told her to try to stretch it out for the triple, but she didn't have the speed to do it. I cost my team the chance to win because I forgot who was running the bases.

The reality is this, recognize the game you're in, do what you need to do to get it done and do it in such a way that your teammates are buying into it. You're going to lose some games, but if you are competing and you are doing everything you can to stay in the game, it will rub off on your team. There are just times when you know you're outmatched and you have to do what you can do and hope for a break. And of course know your limitations, don't ruin the strategy by ending the game on a moment of over enthusiasm. Great Bosses do the best they can under the circumstances with a positive attitude and enthusiasm. BossHoles do the wrong things at the wrong time and ruin their team's chance for success.

When I talk about managing your team, managing your process and playing the way that you want to play, this is what I am talking about. You have to create a basic strategy of how you want to organize your team to succeed, but then there's the actual competition or performance of your work and the many different choices to be made each day. Within those choices you will find your leadership. Setting the tone for your team and leading your team is more than the tactical strategies of putting the right player in the right place and calling the right pitch and running the right defensive play, pitching the batter to exploit their weaknesses and all those kind of tactical issues; it is your respect for the game and the process. Do you play the game with respect for the game and do you play with respect for your opponent, as well as the umpires and the sport itself?

In the heat of battle during a competitive event, your character will be revealed. There are certain rules that you have as a team, and if you're consistent in adhering to those rules and you're consistent to your behavior, your behaviors will be in alignment with your strategy. If your strategy and behavior are aligned, then whether or not you win the tournament or the game, you will succeed in developing the right behaviors, the right attitudes, and the right skill sets to be successful in the future.

Out of respect for the game, a team should have rules such as no mocking of other players, no rudeness to the umpires, no mocking the other team. The team result is more important than individual statistics. Players are here for the team effort, not to build up their own stats. Most importantly, you have to have fun playing this game. You want to play hard and have fun, but approach the game in a way where you're going to compete every single play. In the business world, how this translates is: How do you treat people, how do you treat the rules, how do you treat the laws, how do you treat the competitors?

Are you out there bad mouthing your competitors, being disrespectful, making your patients or your customers wait longer than they need to, not alerting when there's a problem, making them sit out there and just wait and wait and wait with no explanation of what's going on? How do you treat people? How do you treat your community? How do you treat your competitors? That is a big part of deciding who you want to be as a team. There are all different kinds of ways that people do this, and some of your competitors will badmouth you and accuse you of things, and you need to decide how you're going to respond to that up front.

You have to constantly have your finger on the pulse of your group, understand when your team is trying too hard, when they're overworked, when they're underworked, and when they're putting in the right kinds of effort. You want to encourage them and reward the strong effort. You want to immediately correct the wrong level of effort. You want to understand what's going on in your business that day and what needs to be done to make today a success. Then you need to create an environment where everyone has the opportunity to succeed, to play their role, to do well and not with fear of failure, but with an engaged, sincere attempt to live up to your vision that you've set for your business.

# Chapter 8:  Vision Mission Values

"**Start with good people, lay out the rules, communicate with your employees, motivate them and reward them. If you do all those things effectively, you can't miss.**" **Lee Iacocca**

How do you create your leadership vision? How do you align your actions to be consistent with your strategy? You've decided how you want to play, you've decided the style of play, the style you want to run, how do you create a vision that allows you to align your daily actions with this strategy? Not surprisingly, there are three different steps you need to take:

1. **Create that vision.**  You have to decide what is important to you, what you are good at, what you stand for, how you want to be known, what it is that you want to achieve in the marketplace, and what it is that you want to be known for.

2. **Internalize the vision.**  When I say internalize it, I mean how do you model the behaviors, how do you document the behaviors required, what actions do you take that will demonstrate alignment with your vision, and what actions can you take that will create a discord and confusion for people?

3.  **Apply the vision** to everything that you do in your business. If the vision is true and is good and is well thought out and is a good strategy for a successful

business, then everything you do should emanate from your vision.

The vision should be a touchstone. A touchstone is a place that is always within an arm's reach. In business this is the set of core values of your business model. The touchstone is your test for genuineness of all your business ideas. The touchstone is where you return to remember what you're doing and why you're doing it and to remind yourself of what's important. To have this touchstone permeate throughout your business, there are certain things that you have to do. Every talk, every document, every bit of advice that you put out to your employees should remind them of the vision, relate to the vision, and tie to the vision. All of your actions should be aligned with the vision. What you say is important, and what you write is important, but what you do trumps everything. Actions always speak louder than words.

You need to be careful to make sure that your behavior models the vision of your business. Even more importantly, does your attitude align? If you're grumpy and grouchy and moaning and whining, it's very difficult for you not to expect your employees to do the same thing. Grumpy, moaning and whining is not the kind of behavior that is going to help your business succeed. On those days when you need to let off steam and grump and groan and whine, do it offsite, out of vision of your employees. Do it away from your customers, and you will find that it's easier to keep your business moving forward.

Once you've created this vision, internalized it, and aligned your behaviors to model those that you want your employees to have, what's the most important thing? You need to communicate it. You need to communicate your vision correctly and you need to do it in a way where people will be engaged and will understand what that vision means. All too often we use fancy words and jargon in business communications. But this jargon is frequently unclear. How do you know if it is unclear? If you asked 100 people what it means, you'd get 100 different answers.

To clearly communicate your vision requires doing three things.

1. **Define:** appeal to their rational minds by explaining what your vision is and why it fits in the marketplace.

2. **Explain:** solidify the vision by appealing to the emotional side of people, which is explaining to them why that is important. Putting it in a context they can understand.

3. **Anchor:** clarify what actions you expect them to take in order to comply with the mission. All policies should be behaviorally anchored to your vision, mission and values.

Let me give you an example from the independent pharmacy business. Assume that you want to focus on providing the best service. So you hire employees and you tell them, "We give good service." But maybe each employee has a different vision of what that means. You should explain why service is important and put it in context for them.

"The large chain stores have longer hours and they have a bigger front end than we do, so we are appealing directly to the customers who want more care, more handholding, more help than what they're likely to get at the chain store. So it's important for us to offer very good service by getting their prescriptions filled quickly, getting their questions answered, and giving them more help than they would get at our competitors."

That appeals to the rational mind to explain why that makes sense. However, it doesn't quite get people excited. So you appeal to the emotional mind, and here's how you do that. "Here's what I mean when I say good service. Imagine your grandmother comes into the pharmacy. She just got two new prescriptions from the doctor. She doesn't know what they're for, she forgot to ask him. She's got six prescription medications at home. She doesn't know if these new ones are different than the old ones, or whether she is supposed to start taking these and stop taking those. When the prescriptions are ready she takes them home. She isn't quite sure what to do so she just takes all eight medications in the morning with her breakfast. The two new meds were supposed to replace two of the six she had at home. Therefore, one week later she falls at home and breaks her hip because of the side effects of these medications. Did your grandmother get the attention she needed? Did she get the pharmacy care she needed?"

Emotionally appealing to your team by personalizing the concept of service to imagine someone they care about can be a powerful motivator. They want to know how what they do impacts real people. It is a way to engage the emotional mind.

The third element of successfully communicating your vision is breaking it down to behaviorally anchored actions. Tell your employees the actionable things they can do. Telling them to give good service is a starting point, but what does giving good service mean? In my retail pharmacy we had three simple rules of behavior.

1. **Acknowledge** every customer within five seconds of them coming to the counter. If you can't help them right away at least say, "Excuse me just a minute. I'm on the phone. I will be right with you in just a second, okay?" You must acknowledge every customer immediately.

2. **Listen** to the customer. Listen for what they're really asking you. Listen for what they don't understand and clarify any errors before they leave the counter. Our job is to discover what they really need, understand what they really want and deliver it on time.

3. **Solve** problems. If there is a problem, notify the customer immediately. Give them an estimate of how long it's going to take to fix and give them the option of coming back later or getting home delivery.

Specifying actions that directly flow from the touchstone of excellent service clarify what good service means. In terms of creating your vision, remember you've got to craft your vision statement around: what is important to your customers, what are you good at, and what you want to stand for. Then you've got to relate everything that you do, every action that you take, every policy that you have to the touchstone.

The behavior that you expect, the behavior that you model, must align with the vision. You must communicate this vision as often as needed by appealing to the rational brain, stimulating the emotional brain and clarifying the simple action steps required. You must describe what you expect to be done to prove you are giving good service. Ultimately your success in the marketplace will revolve around whether or not your vision is a good vision. Is it something that needs to be done? Do people need better service than they're getting from the alternatives?

Great Bosses align their businesses with good visions. BossHoles look for selfish gain. Good visions have the chance to succeed but only if they're merged with quality actions. It's not enough to have a good idea. You have to have a good idea and follow through with the appropriate actions to make that idea happen. There are a million good ideas that never get acted on. There are a lot of okay ideas that succeed, because someone got off the couch and actually started doing it. Along the way, they learned how to do it better, and then they refined it, and then pretty soon they had a successful business built around this idea. It is never just the vision that creates success. It is the vision merged with the appropriate level of action. Understand that the real world doesn't always work out like you plan. In fact, it rarely does. If you're providing good leadership by staying in the game and doing things that should be done the right way, at least you have a chance to succeed.

Let me give you an example of this. After seeing how a lot of different fast pitch softball teams were practicing deceptive recruiting tactics I decided to promote a different approach. Many coaches were promising kids anything to get them on their team and then basically never giving them play time. Some CoachHoles would entice kids to sign with them only to bring college players back for the big tournaments and sit these kids on the bench. This would win games for the coach but deprive their young players of the playing time necessary to get the college coach exposure they needed to get recruited. We decided to take a different approach with my 16 and under team when we intentionally brought on 15 versatile athletes, all of whom could play three positions.

We organized a team where we intentionally had a lot of really good players that could start for a lot of competitive teams. But we guaranteed them that we would play four out of every five games. They would each play two games at what was considered their primary position and one each at their secondary positions. We made sure everybody got the same amount of innings. Then we set it up so that when we got to an ultra-competitive tournament, players would compete for spots based on performance to decide who would play in the elimination games. I felt this was important, because no one knows with any certainty the position these kids were going to play in college. I felt strongly that versatility and flexibility would be an advantage as they progressed through the recruiting cycle. I felt that college coaches would say, "This kid can do multiple kinds of things. That's going to be valuable to me."

All the players bought into it. They agreed to come on board under those conditions, and it was going pretty well until the middle of the winter season. Some of the moms started complaining, because their daughters were sitting out a game. Of course, every daughter was sitting out a game every five, because we had predefined it, but that became a perceived slight to their children, when they were sitting out.

The team started to have problems with players not playing up to their potential. We would get into games and not perform as well as I thought we should have. So at one point we decided to get away from the parents, to get off by ourselves and re-commit to the plan. We went to a ropes course, and did a lot of team building activities. We sat down and talked about committing to the team, committing to a strategy and basically asked each player to commit to play for the team and do whatever the team needed them to do to succeed, and a very interesting thing happened.

Six of the players quit, and we were down to nine players. Those nine became so close and so committed that, by getting rid of the players that weren't really committed to the team strategy, they just became incredibly powerful. They played together, they played hard, and they fought through whatever came along. As we added players through the summer before we went out to the national tournament, this group of kids played like they were invincible. They were not afraid of anybody. They played incredibly hard. Even though we lost some talented players that wouldn't commit to the team concept and we didn't have all the talent we needed, we competed and we ended up finishing fifth at nationals out of 84 teams. They were an incredibly amazing group of kids, and as I said before, my all-time favorite team.

I will admit I was surprised when six kids quit. I admit that I was discouraged and wondered whether I should have given up and folded the team. Going into January with only nine players rostered and with a lack of pitching depth was a huge risk. My assistant coaches were ready to quit and admit that our experiment failed. But BossHoles give up when bad things happen. BossHoles cut and run and blame others for their failures. And I refused to be a BossHole. If I had given up and folded I would have missed out on an amazing experience that was filled with moments I now treasure. Great Bosses don't give up when times get tough. Great Bosses dig in and figure out a way to work through trouble.

The message here is that for a team to succeed, everybody has to buy into what the team is doing. A small core of people with tremendous buy-in and dedication can take you a heck of a lot longer and farther than a bigger group of people when only two-thirds of them buy in. The negative energy created by the whiners and complainers and the ones that don't play by your rules will drag down the entire team.

Your vision and your mission must be wrapped in and infused with your core beliefs. The vision should answer: Where do we stake our claim? Where will we achieve our greatness? What do we want to be known for? The mission explains: How are we going to go about doing it? The core values declare: What are the core principles we will use to guide our actions?

The reason you need all three is that the vision sets the tone, the mission sets the strategy, but the core values drive the hundreds of little decisions that determine whether or not you will be successful. The core beliefs that I have settled on, that I use in every one of my businesses, in my courses, in anything that I teach, are three things.

1. **Do** the **right** thing, even when no one is watching, even when you don't feel like it, you do what's right.
2. **Treat** others as they deserve to be treated.
3. Strive for **excellence.**

My viewpoint is that if you're not trying to be great, don't apply to be on my team. I want people who want to be great. I don't want people that are okay with being mediocre. If you're okay with mediocre, please go work for one of my competitors. This is how you take your strategy, turn it into a vision, frame it into a mission and wrap it around your core values that will help guide you in the little decisions that you have to make every day.

Let me give you a pharmacy example. Our pharmacy was next door to a Subway sandwich shop. My wife, who was my pharmacy manager, noticed that the employees were coming into work in the morning with a large soda from Subway and then going back all day long and getting free refills for that soda. When she asked one of the employees what they were doing, they said, "It's free refills so we just buy a cup in the morning and then refill it all day long. I get like ten sodas." She looked at them and said, "That's dishonest. If you're going to do that, don't bring that soda into my store. Free refill means when you're in Subway having your sandwich and you want more to drink, go have it. It doesn't mean I've got 24 hours' worth of soda free. It's a refill in the context of a visit to the establishment, not for 12 visits."

They immediately stopped doing it. What did that communicate to my employees? If it's not right, don't do it. Even little tiny things that are not right need to be fixed immediately, because then people learn that it is important that I do things right. Don't be afraid to tell people what's right and what's wrong. Probably the biggest problem we have in America today is the fact that schools are not allowed to tell kids what's right and wrong anymore. If they're not going to learn in school, they need to learn while they work for you. Because if you allow them to do stuff that isn't right, you're basically saying that's okay and that even though I have these rules and even though that's unfair, even though that's dishonest, I'm going to ignore it. Ignoring it is the same thing as making it your policy. Employees stealing soda from the local Subway restaurant had no direct impact on the profits of our pharmacy but it was in direct conflict with our core values. Doing what's right even when no one is watching, treating others as they deserve to be treated and striving for excellence is a simple set of guardrails to help you determine what to do at any given time.

Let me give you an example of the difference between the chain practice of pharmacy and the independent practice of pharmacy and how this difference manifests in the BossHole effect® Chains thrive on systems and processes attempting to create the identical experience in each store. Imagine a case where a woman picks up and pays for her prescription and leaves the store to go home. At home she discovers that she actually ordered the wrong medication. She unintentionally ordered the one she had plenty of and not the one she was running out of. So she returns to the store and asks for a refund because now she doesn't have the money to buy the prescription she really needs.

For all you non-pharmacists out there let me explain that a pharmacy is not allowed to take a prescription back and re-dispense the medication to another patient. Once the drug has left the control of the pharmacy the chain of custody has been broken and the pharmacist cannot guarantee the product is unadulterated. A request for a refund at the local chain drug store will be typically met with an apology and a declaration that, "We are not allowed to take medication back." In addition, because of cash handling protocols and internal security procedures a pharmacist can possibly be fired for offering a discount or refund. The net effect of this system wide policy is that employees are afraid to break a rule and customers don't have a reasonable request honored. That is the genesis of the BossHole Effect®.

Independent drug stores thrive on providing a unique experience for each customer. My goal as a Good independent Boss was to do what was in the best interest of the customer. Even if I had to give a refund and then throw the drug away, I was going to help out the customer. I would always consider, "How would I want to be treated if I was a customer?" I would love it if someone would just solve the darn problem and cut me some slack. So in our store we routinely gave refunds when it was appropriate. It solidified a bond with that customer that was unbreakable despite all the $20 coupons the chains were mailing out. The simple act of human kindness in helping another person who needs help is the essence of pharmacy care. You become an excellent customer service organization by knowing when to take the customer's side and give her what she needs. If a BossHole creates a fear of breaking rules rather than a culture of customer service the knucklehead will destroy the ability of the team to be great.

Once you have crafted your strategy, you've created your vision and mission statement, how do you put your team in a position to succeed? What do you do as a leader that puts them in a position to succeed? Leadership is not about being the person with all the answers. It's really about getting your organization to take the right actions. So, how do you create an environment where your team has the ability to do their best and to compete and to succeed?

There are three kinds of authority within an organization.

1. **Positional** authority is based on your title. You're the vice president, I'm the district manager. In that case the higher title has the power.

2. **Organizational** authority is based on your level in the organization chart. You have authority over me because your organization has decreed it so. The organizational chart says that Mary, Tom and Louis report to Frieda. You can tell who has the authority based on how high up the organizational chart they are. The organizational chart may or may not be based on titles and positional authority. However, there is another kind of authority that is based on performance.

3.  **Performance** based authority occurs when you have the authority because you are the one who can get things done. Regardless of what your job title is or the organizational chart shows, you're a leader because you do things that make people want to emulate you and do it the way that you do it.

There can be people with positional and organizational authority who are BossHoles and don't deserve the titles that they have. There are people who are Great Bosses who have no title. And there are Great Bosses who also have the positional authority and the organizational authority to make stuff happen. Great Bosses honestly earn the performance-based authority. BossHoles usually lack any performance-based authority.

Small businesses and small organizations succeed based on the performance-based leadership of a Great Boss. Employees willingly follow a Great Boss because he/she is the kind of person they want to follow. This is the essence of leading by example and is a powerful motivation force that can be used to energize an entire organization.

What is it about leaders, these "natural leaders", that makes people want to follow them? It has a lot to do with their personal values, their work ethic, the way that they treat people, how they act and how they model certain behaviors. Ultimately, successful leaders are good at balancing the three "C's." I know I have explained this multiple times earlier in this book but these concepts are so important I am going to restate it again for you here.

1. The first "C" is that of a **coach**. The coach is the guy or gal who works individually with you to improve your skill set, to teach you how to hit better, field better, run faster, jump higher, and how to get more of your abilities to manifest in performance. That's what coaches do. So every powerful performance-based leader does things that involve coaching the people that they need to perform for them.

2. The second "C" is having the bravery to **command**. This means understanding when you need to step in and right the ship, when you need to step in and provide a firm moment of leadership that stops the team from going in the wrong direction and starts everything moving in the right direction. This is perhaps the most difficult thing to learn and can be made much easier by defining your core values in a way that they will help guide your actions when these moments come up.

3. The third "C" is to **create** an environment where your people can excel at fulfilling your vision and mission. This is all about the coaching you do, the commands you give and the way in which you treat people.

A critical balance point for you will be developing and training employees to do what you want them to do, in the way you want them to do it. Let me use a real world example from community pharmacy practice.

Assume that your goal was to cross train every employee in the various workflow positions. If the new technician Susie is not very good at inputting prescriptions into the computer yet you might schedule her for Thursday afternoons to train, when it's typically slow. She needs to learn how to input the prescriptions properly, do the insurance properly, do the billing properly and all that. She works hard during her other shifts and looks forward to the opportunity to get onto the computer and start inputting prescriptions. Normally that's fine. Thursdays are slow.

The pharmacy typically receives its warehouse order on Thursday morning. You have your main input technician, Nancy, scheduled to put the order away leaving an opening for Susie to perform the inputting function. However, on this particular Thursday a third technician has called in sick, and it's a busier day than normal. All of a sudden the customer lines are too long and customer wait times have become unacceptable. Susie the new tech isn't able to keep up with inputting the prescriptions. She's not accurate enough and she's not fast enough. Here is your Command challenge as a Boss. You can follow the daily plan even though it is hurting customer service, by saying, "Well, I made a staffing plan and I know Susie is looking forward to inputting, so I don't want to hurt her feelings,"

Or you can take Command and make a decision that will honor your commitment to good service by saying, "Everyone stop what you're doing. Nancy, get back on the number one computer. Susie, go get this line down. Everyone stop putting the order away, come over here and help fill prescriptions. Once everyone steps in, gets the lines down, gets the workflow organized, and gets all the customers taken care of we can go back to what you were doing without damaging service."

BossHoles stick with a plan even though it fails to support the mission. Great Bosses adjust on the fly to get the right things done at the right time. Many bosses are afraid to do that. They abdicate their responsibility as leaders. Great Bosses step in and preserve the vision, mission and values of the business. If your strategy is based on giving excellent customer service, making your customers wait behind 15 people so that Susie can learn how to use the computer is not good customer service. If that happens you need to rotate out of that bad situation and fix it; then you can go back to training when it's slower. It's not offensive, it's not mean. It's the right thing to do and it's helping treat your customers the way they deserve to be treated. It's helping you maintain your excellent reputation of getting them in and out in a hurry.

Part of knowing when to step in and take control is recognizing where you are in this process of leadership. Are you currently in training mode? Are you operating in routine mode or crisis mode? Are you coaching, commanding or creating the environment? Great Bosses know when to lead, when to give a pat on the back and when to apply a kick in the butt.

When you're operating in a training mode you're allowing somebody who isn't quite trained yet to practice their skills. How do you behave so that you get the best performance out of the trainee? If every time she makes a mistake she gets reprimanded, she will become afraid to make mistakes and therefore they stop trying. That is how BossHoles act to undermine the confidence of their staff. Great Bosses understand when they're in the Coaching mode and training for the future. They understand when to apply gentle taps to the brakes to get a trainee to slow down and when to gently apply the accelerator to get a trainee to move a little faster. Great Bosses say something like, "Hey, this is good, but here's one thing you could do that would make it go a little faster." BossHoles say something like, "This isn't right do it over again." Training costs are a significant expense to every business. Too many businesses under appreciate the true cost developing a high performance team and underestimate the real cost of disengaging their workforce. Engaged employees keep trying to get better. Ultimately, better employees produce better performance if they are led by a Great Boss.

When operating in routine business mode your staff should be trained to do what they are doing. Therefore sloppiness or inaccuracy should not be tolerated. If you can see a little bit of something that they're missing in their process that would make them better at what they do, you need to point it out. If you don't demand it to be done right, it won't get done right. It's hard for employees to know what your vision is if you don't frequently remind them about what is important to you.

Let me give an example: Assume that your goal is to train softball players on how to field ground balls. You're going to hit a variety of ground balls to each player and work on their fielding mechanics. One player fields all the ground balls and makes all the throws but you notice that her footwork is not correct. She takes a drop step backwards instead of going forward. She doesn't move correctly, her first step is not towards the ball. She's not centering her body up on the ball. She's off balance or she's just stabbing at it. Even though she made the plays, her form is not correct. Yes, she fielded the ground ball and threw it to first, but if you allow the weaknesses in her mechanics to go unchecked, it will cost the team at some point. There will come a time when it matters in a game, when she's tired and her form will breakdown. She will make an error or not get to a ball because she didn't have the right footwork. It is your responsibility as a Great Boss to properly train your team.

The same thing happens in a business such as pharmacy. There's a way to do it quicker, faster, more efficiently. There's a way to fill prescriptions so that you double check and improve accuracy. There's a way to make sure the right drug is in the right bottle. There are processes that you have to follow. And there are skills and habits that make for a more efficient and productive process. When it is a slow day you can get by with a bit of disorganization but on the really busy days, a sloppy process will produce poor service. And the only way your team will learn a good process is if you take the time to teach them how you want it done.

Part of being a leader is recognizing when you're training, when you're perfecting somebody's routine, and when you are in a crisis mode. When you're at crunch time and the game is afoot, or the championship is on the line, you need to deliver. You've got no room for error. There is a very short time line. There's no opportunity to experiment. There's no opportunity to try something. You have to have tried everything before you get to the game that matters. You have to know how people are going to respond and how they are going to perform.

Great Bosses start with the end in mind. In the toughest environment, in the busiest day, in an overload situation where you've got twice as much business and not enough people, what are the critical skills that need to be done at the intake window, at the input window, at the filling station, at the checking station, at the handout station? Those are the skills you must have in your mind. Those are the skills you have to train for. Those are the skills you have to make sure people are performing from muscle memory. Unless your teammates were born perfect they will have to have failed at something and corrected their deficiencies so that when a calamity happens in the big game, they are ready to perform. You can't just hope and pray that it will all work out. Being a Great Boss means knowing what needs to be done, what it takes to get there and helping your people build those skills before they need to use them. The big three leadership skills are: Coaching, that is, teaching the skills they need. Commanding, that is, being decisive when you need to, and making the tough decisions. And Creating, that is, fostering the environment that allows people to do what they do best and allows the team to perform to the utmost of their abilities.

In the sports world, if you've trained your people and you've got good players, most of the time they'll go out and compete. The boss doesn't have to make that many decisions in the course of the game. The players can take care of themselves. However, there comes a critical juncture in each championship run when key decisions need to be made. Deciding who's going to pitch, who's going to get the big at-bat, and the defensive strategy are decisions the leader must make. The Great Boss earns respect, by making the right decision that's in the best interest of his team, at the moment it needs to be made. Ultimately the boss's job is to put her team in the best possible position to succeed.

The best leaders create a team that is more powerful than the sum of the talents of the individual players. BossHoles make the wrong decisions or procrastinate until the team is demoralized.

Let me give you an example: My team was in the middle of a championship tournament when a dispute broke out amongst the parents. There were complaints that a certain player got more playing time than another player, and then it spun out of control. Pretty soon several parents were barking at each other on the sidelines. I was on the field trying to get these players to win and to play together in a championship fashion, and I was getting flak from this group of parents about "Why did she get to play this inning and my daughter didn't?"

There was basically a critical point going into championship weekend when I had a bunch of parents that were frustrated and angry about their own selfish playing time issues. It was starting to spill over onto the field, because the kids knew everything that was bothering their parents. So after we finished the games that day, I called a parent meeting. I put all the parents in the room. I had my wife take all the kids out to dinner.

I pulled out my checkbook and said, "Listen to me very carefully. Your daughters are in a position to win a national championship. I don't know if this is anything that they will ever have the opportunity to do again, but I know we have the talent to win this thing and we have the players to win this thing. And if you guys will just stay out of it and let them play, we will win this thing. So here's the deal – any of you who are not happy with play time and who don't think that I am managing the right way are free to think that, but you're free to think it at home. If you're not going to shut up and watch the games, then get the hell out of here. I will write you a check for whatever it cost you to get on a plane and get out of town tonight. But you are not going to show up on that field and poison the attitude around this team or prevent these kids from having the opportunity to win. If you want what's best for the team, stay and watch the game. If you don't, leave now. I don't care what you're arguing about, if you want to go out to a bowling alley and yell at each other, fine, but you have no right to get in these kids' heads and keep them from playing at their best." Then I left the room.

The next day, the team played their fannies off but ended up suffering a loss and dropping into the loser's bracket late Saturday night. Obviously, I would have preferred to win but after that loss I called the kids together for a chat. We had uncharacteristically made a few errors that cost us the game. A BossHole would have chewed them out and benched some players. I kept it short and just said, "Everybody get a good night sleep because we are going to have to win three games tomorrow." The next morning we got up and had breakfast together as a team. By keeping the mood light and the energy positive I prodded the team to play hard and have fun. We came back and won all three games on Sunday, winning the national tournament. Had I not shielded my players from the negative energy of others, they would never have succeeded. Never be afraid to show leadership when it needs to be shown. Let your decisions be guided by your values.

There's a time when the leader has to step up and be a leader. You cannot abdicate the responsibility for running your business to anyone else. You can't. You have to have the guts to be a leader, and leadership requires three roles. You need to be a coach, you need to command, and you need to create an environment where your team is engaged in the process and you're getting the best possible performance out of their abilities.

# Chapter 9: Casting Your Team of Characters

**"The strength of the team is each individual member. The strength of each member is the team." Phil Jackson, Basketball Coach**

Once you've developed your strategy and you understand what a leader has to do to enforce that strategy and to lead the team to success, you are faced with the task of how you assemble a team to accomplish your strategy. This is a crucial process that will only succeed when you clearly understand what your team must do to succeed using the strategy you're trying to use. If you're saying that your strategy is based on speed, base stealing and putting the ball in play, and then you go out and recruit a bunch of big, slow, power hitters who strike out a lot, then you're not matching the players to your strategy.

If you say, "I'm going to have excellent customer service and be better than anyone else in town," and then you hire grouchy, lazy, snippy people, you're not going to achieve your strategy. You're not going to be successful. You have to find teammates with the skill sets that you need in order for them to do what you want them to do, and in the way you need them to do it.

The first step in this process is to understand what the attributes are that you are looking for in a teammate. Are you looking for a certain knowledge base, a certain skill set, a certain attitude? Must they have certain abilities? What are the things that are actually important for you, and more specifically, for the job you're asking your employees to do? It is more likely that you're going to employ average people who need to be developed, than you're going to be able to find these pre-made superstars. When you do find them, it's great. Obviously that lets your team move up the ranks faster, but you just can't count on that as a long-term strategy. You're still going to need to round out your team with people that can do a really good job, and for most of those folks, you're going to have to teach them how to do it.

There are several hiring strategies you can deploy. If you were assembling a baseball team, you would need a catcher, a pitcher, a first baseman, second baseman, third baseman, shortstop and outfielders. Once your starting nine were chosen you would need to complete your roster with role players. Do you want to have two catchers? Do you want to have two third basemen? Do you want to have a couple of utility players that can play anywhere you want them to play?

Those are all decisions that you need to make to play the game in the style of play that you want to play it. Are you going to be a team that plays for the three-run home run? If so, then you're going to want a couple of big boppers sitting on the bench, a left-hander and a right-hander to deliver the big hit for you.

You have to understand your strategy and you have to understand what knowledge, skills, abilities and attitudes teammates must have for that strategy to succeed. In addition, there are negative behavior attributes that are unacceptable. The most practical selection strategy is to use these negative attributes as knockout items. If you interview somebody with any of those attributes, it's a knockout - they don't get the job. They don't get to be on the team, regardless of their skill set. You should not care even if they can type 100 words a minute or appear to be a perfect fit for the skill you need. If they are a snarly, snarky, nasty person, or trigger one of your knockout attributes you don't want them around.

You need to decide what the knockout questions are for you. What are the things you simply will not tolerate in your employees? Put that list in writing and keep it in your pocket and as you're interviewing, as you're doing reference checks, as you're asking people who worked with this person what they're like. Don't hire people with knockout issues.

A more difficult task is determining the things an employee must be able to do or show the capacity to do. There are certain people who may not have any experience but could be spectacular after two months with you. There are other people who have a lot of experience at being mediocre. If you accept mediocre, you're telling the rest of your team that mediocre is okay. If you accept less than good, you're telling the rest of your team that even though you say you want to be great, you're allowing somebody who is not even good to stay on the team.

Looking for the skills that you need and filtering for the behaviors and attitudes that you don't want will help you be more accurate in selecting players for your team and will help you make less hiring errors. Still, the reality is you will make errors. You will have a loser who sneaks through. You will have a teammate that doesn't perform as advertised. The fallback strategy is to ruthlessly practice what I call the sheepdog theory of management.

I learned this from a sheep farmer in Ireland when my wife and I visited there a few years back. This farmer did a demonstration of his sheepdogs. These two dogs could move sheep up and down the hill. They could get a herd of 50 or 60 sheep to move where they wanted them to go with their body language. Just by whistling the farmer could get these two dogs to move the sheep up and down the hill, take them to a better grazing area, bring them down at the end of the day and do whatever he needed them to do. It was just fascinating to watch the dogs work together. Each dog had his own whistle, and the dogs knew which whistle was for him. After the event, I asked the guy, "How long does it take you to teach a dog to do this?" He told me that it took about two years for them to get fully trained. I then asked, "Is every dog capable of learning this?" He said, "No, there are some dogs that just don't get it. If I work with a dog for two weeks and he doesn't get it, then I give him away as a pet, because he's not going to get it."

As I thought back on my career of hiring and firing employees over the years, a light bulb went on. The two-week trial period is a good model to use, because it plays out with humans too, not just dogs. Most employees are excited to take on a new job. They're trying to do their best. They're trying to show they belong. They want to do well. They're a little nervous. They're a little scared of how you're going to react, but they are there trying hard to be good. So, if someone is with you for two weeks and she's terrible, in my experience, that's as good as she's going to get.

If you find out within the first couple weeks that they can't get there on time, they can't seem to catch on, they can't seem to do anything right, then they need to go be somebody else's problem. They need to be playing for somebody else. You need to move them out quickly, since again, it communicates to your team there's stuff that needs to get done, and if you can't do it, you're out. She could be a delightful person but if she can't do what you need her to do, she has got to go. Part of being a good leader is to acknowledge when you've made a bad hire and correct that mistake as soon as possible. It doesn't mean you have to be a jerk about it but it needs to be done for the sake of the team.

Another part of assembling a team in the business world is to consider problem-solving style. In addition to the traditional skill sets like the ability to run a computer, do billing, or handle customers nicely, there's an entire other dimension to running a high-value team that doesn't get a lot of attention. Research by Inscape Publishing developed the Team Dimensions profile, which classifies each person by their team roles. There are five basic styles.

1. **Creator**: People who generate new ideas and fresh points of view. They prefer to live in the land of possibilities. They thrive on innovation and unique solutions.

2. **Advancer:** Team members who communicate new ideas and move them forward. They focus on the personal interactive world of feelings and relationships. They manage the human side of issues and enjoy building enthusiasm.

3. **Refiner:** Individuals who analyze a solution for flaws or enjoy revising a plan are refiners. They focus on the objective world of analytics. They use logic and a systematic approach to make sure that ideas are sound before moving them forward.

4. **Executor**: People who deliver concrete results and love to implement are executors. They make sure that everything gets accomplished and they pay attention to the details.

5. **Flexer**: These individuals are a combination of the other styles and have an equal preference for most or all of the roles. They can adapt to the needs of the team.

No role is better or more important than another role when it comes to moving teamwork forward. The most effective teams have members who do what they do best and who allow the other team members to do what they do best. A team without a balance of styles will get bogged down by the weakness of that style.

Within a workgroup, you need team members that have a variety of these skills and you need to know who should perform which task. The creative types will always think up new ideas, but they spend their time thinking and creating and not necessarily getting a lot done. The prioritizing people, the Advancers, will be great at prioritizing your list, but they're not always good at making sure that's actually what we should be doing. The Refiner people are good at saying, "Here's what you can't do, here's why you can't do it." So if they're in charge or they're the only ones on task, nothing gets done because they can always see why it won't work.

The Executor people are the ones who say, "Just tell me what to do and I'll do it." Executor types will work very hard at doing the wrong thing and get lots of the wrong things done, if they are not part of a well-rounded team. So the focal point for teambuilding, rather than just job proficiency skills, is to also look at how do they approach work, how do they add to your decision-making team?

As a business owner, you are automatically part of a problem-solving team whose role is to solve problems for your customers. There is a process defined by the Team Dimensions profile that dramatically improves the effectiveness of teams by 300% to 800%. The process goes something like this:

When there is a problem to be solved, everybody on the team jumps in and brainstorms and says, "What is the problem, what should we do?" and everybody puts ideas up on the board. At this stage of it, the brainstorming stage, there's no filtering. Everybody chips in and everybody throws the ideas out. There's no hierarchy. There's no somebody's right, somebody's wrong. It's just an idea.

At the second page of the process, the Advancers review the list and say, "Here are the ones that look like they're most likely to be most successful solutions. So let's pick the top three or four choices."

Then the Refiner types review those choices and say, "That's a good choice except for it's going to run into a problem when … and how do we fix that?" That's when the Creator types need to step in and say, "We could do it this way at that time, and that will fix the problem." So once the Refiners have pointed out what won't work, then it is the role of the Creator to jump in and say, "Here's a creative solution to that."

Then the group again looks at the process to see if there are any more problems. If there are problems, the team goes through another iteration, but if not, they say, "Let's move forward with this plan." That's when the Executors step in and say, "I will get it done." Great Bosses will employ those four functions within their problem-solving process. BossHoles make all the key decisions without a good process. Even if you are the only employee in your company, you still have to follow the process. Since many solo entrepreneurs are the creative type they may have to build a problem solving network that includes people outside of their organization. They will want to run their ideas by people that will help them prioritize, people that will help them fact check and make sure it will actually work, and then have people that pound the work out so that it will actually get done.

Great Bosses want to create an environment where people can succeed, where people can do what they do best. Obviously then, you need to know what they do best, put the employee in the position to their best, and then help them feel that they are an important part of your group. This is so important that it bears repeating from an earlier chapter. There are really only three things that determine whether or not people will stay working for you and will do the right things for you. It comes down to answering these simple questions:

1. Is what I do **important**? Is the work that I am doing something that really needs to be done?

2. Am I **good at** what I do? If I don't feel like I'm good at what I do, I really don't like to do it, and I really don't see the point.

3. Does my **boss recognize** and appreciate that I'm good at it?

If those three conditions are met, people will be engaged; they will be enthusiastic and do a great job. If any of them are not met, people are going to be undermining your team effort. It is not the rate of pay. It is not the hours. It is not the size of the business that drives employees to be great. It's very simply: Am I good at what I do? Is what I do important? Does my boss know that I'm good at it and appreciate me?

The secret to success as an employer is to understand this critical issue with regards to employee retention. People join good companies, but they quit bad bosses. BossHoles end up chasing off good people and deteriorating the average talent of their organization. Good people won't work for a BossHole unless they need to. Bad people may like working for a BossHole because they can remain employed as long as they do what they are told every day. People who are excited to join the company because they love what the company stands for align with the vision and the way they do things. But if the boss doesn't model the right behaviors, doesn't treat them with respect, doesn't appreciate that they're good at their jobs, they're going to leave, even though it's a good company. The cost of employee turnover is hellacious. Losing good people is something you never want to do. Losing bad people is something you always want to do. Eliminating BossHoles is a cost saver and a morale booster for any team.

The team problem-solving process as defined by the Team Dimensions profile research has shown that teams that follow the simple problem-solving system are more productive, faster, and make better decisions than other teams. Therefore when you're building a team and selecting people, look not just at their skills but what type of problem-solving style they have.

Do they mesh with your style? Do they strengthen your weaknesses? Go back through your memory banks and think of the people that you really liked working with and how productive you were. Which styles mesh with yours the best? Because if you don't understand why someone behaves the way they do, and you don't understand how important a Creator, an Advancer, a Refiner, and an Executor are then you won't understand how to maximize the productivity of your team.

You will miscast them into a role in which they do not perform well instead of putting them in a role at which they can excel. When you're organizing your team, you have to have a strategy about how you're going to fill the slots. Are you going to go out and get your pitchers first, and then fill in with position players? Do you need an input tech and a filling tech, and then pick up my front staff later? You need somebody who can swing between the front and the filling position. What exactly is it that you want and need, and then in your leadership team, your supervisors, your decision-makers on your team, do you have all of the roles that you'd need to be played in the team dimensions profile?

Again the key to success is going to be action. In addition to their technical skill set and their problem-solving styles, three elements remain that you must incorporate into your team assembly process: Attitude, Effort and Character. If they can't do all of this with the right attitude, you don't want them. If they won't put in a solid effort, you don't want them. If they have a great attitude and give great effort they will likely be able to grow into whatever job you want them to do.

The third element, of course, is character. Are they honest? Do they have integrity? Do they treat others with respect? If they can't treat others with respect, even though they have the technical skills, you don't want them. Throughout my long career in business, anytime I have ignored character or overlooked a character flaw because there were some great technical skills, I've paid for it dearly. Here's the problem. When it comes to assembling your team and keeping your team productive, a key element is eliminating people that are damaging your team. And sometimes, kicking somebody off your team is the best way to improve performance.

I had a situation with my pharmacy where we were buying another competitor that was near us, closing it down and bringing their business into our store. This was going to mean about a 25% volume increase. My management team got together, and we decided we needed to increase staff and organize the workflow to handle the extra load. We decided that the safest bet would be to bring in a new person to help us with inputting prescriptions, especially during those first three to four months. So we hired a person and brought her in to do inputting. This meant that instead of having two inputters, we had three. Instantaneously, our productivity deteriorated. We became slower, there were more problems, more errors and the lines got longer. It made absolutely no sense that adding an extra person could screw up workflow so badly. This was going on for several weeks until I figured out what was happening. In the pharmacy world, every time you hit a snag, it slows everything down, and your people are being pulled off the line to handle problems which causes further delays.

I had a video system in our store so I was able to videotape the line and videotape the input stations and see what was going on. When I pulled the tape on this new lady and watched her work for 45 minutes, she began with a stack of probably 50 prescriptions to input, and at the end of 40 minutes, she had entered and filled one prescription. To make it worse, she pretended to be on the phone. She was walking around talking to the main inputter, the filling tech and interrupting the pharmacist. She was not only avoiding her job, but she was distracting everybody else from doing their jobs. An amazing thing happened. We let her go and the lines went back to being ten minutes, and the process improved.

So understand that sometimes we make assumptions that more is better, and sometimes we make assumptions that people couldn't possibly be that out of line with expectations. But the reality is that sometimes you make a bad hire, and the quicker you reverse it, the better off your team is going to be, the better off your customers are going to be, and you will maintain alignment with your goals, your objectives, and your team.

Please don't take this last story as an endorsement to act like a BossHole. A BossHole terminates someone in a way that is demeaning and punitive. I believe that you always need to treat people fairly. Most people that you end up letting go deserve to be treated in such a way that you leave them with their dignity intact. After all, it is partly your fault as the person who made the hiring decision for putting them in a position to fail. However, you need to still identify who is a character problem, an attitude problem, an effort problem, and who is a lack of ability problem. The way I do this is by returning to my previously stated values that I believe there are only three kinds of people in the world.

There are good people; these good people get up every morning trying to do good things. They may not always do good things, and sometimes they may do something bad, but a good person is trying to do good work. When they do something wrong, they realize it and they fix it. There are bad people. Bad people wake up every day trying to wreak havoc. They really enjoy being bad. They do bad stuff. They cheat. They lie. They steal. They avoid work. They create problems. They sabotage your efforts. Those people sometimes do very good things. Some of them can be excellent workers when you're watching. Some of them can be very fast and efficient, but they will always revert to their evil character when given the opportunity.

The third kind of person is typically a young person that really hasn't formed yet. They can go either way to become good or bad. So when you're considering employees you must make a critical decision. Is this is a good person who just messed something up and can learn from it and get better? Is this a bad person who maybe can do some things really well, but at her core she is dishonest, she has an evil character, she is a saboteur? Or is this somebody who is just young and hasn't figured it out yet; so she is still someone we can train to behave the way we want her to behave?

If she is a good person, you try to keep her in the business. If she's a bad person, get rid of her as fast as possible. If she's a "haven't decided yet" person, then try to train her but if you give her enough time, and she persists with a bad attitude, bad effort, or bad character, then get rid of her. You can always find somebody better than that. You can't afford to get rid of good people. So you need to know the difference between a good person and a bad person. Great Bosses attract and retain good people and give them the freedom to do their jobs. You will never be 100% accurate in your choices. But with the enormous benefit of hindsight it is easy to see that when I have not followed my own rules it has cost me dearly.

I will punctuate this notion with an example of a technician that had tremendous technical skills. She was a very fast typist, very sharp, excellent at solving billing problems, articulate, charming when she wanted to be, and could do a lot of work in a hurry. Then negative behaviors started showing up. She was spending a lot time on the phone, filling prescriptions for her family members that may or may not have ever gotten paid for, and when I walked past her, she would get really quiet.

She got frequent personal phone calls from a boyfriend all day long. All were little signs that something wasn't kosher. I knew something wasn't right but I always found an excuse for not taking any action because she was very fast and efficient when she wanted to be. But it turns out she was dishonest and devious. She was on best behavior when I was watching but behind my back did the exact opposite.

One day I received a letter from one of our key senior residential assisted living accounts that they were transferring their business to a different pharmacy. When I called to investigate the reason it all revolved around this young lady not properly serving the account. This prompted me to investigate further and discover several other acts of unethical behavior that led to her termination. The moral of the story is that thoughts become action, actions become habits and these habits illuminate character. Failure to eliminate people with poor character from your team always undermines the success of your team.

What I'm saying is, if you're looking at just the technical skills, looking at just whether the employee is nice, you may overlook the fact that, at their core, they do evil stuff and they're dishonest. If you allow a dishonest person to stay, it will poison your team. If you allow an unethical person to stay, it will eventually poison your team. I've been burned multiple times in my career by bad people with evil intent, but you have to decide how to deal with that and not let it poison your relationship with the good people. The number one complaint I hear from employees about their bosses is that they aren't quick enough to pull the trigger on bad people. Everybody knows this person's a knucklehead, and the boss just doesn't man up and fire them. The truth is that the day you terminate the knucklehead, morale improves.

Remember that I use three simple values to guide my actions: do what is right, treat other people the way you want to be treated and strive for excellence. There can be somebody that all your employees like and they think is a nice person who might be doing something unethical or immoral or dishonest. Your private correctional discussions with this employee would be confidential. So if you have to fire that person, you run the risk of having everybody on your team say, "You got rid of poor Mary Jo, and she was my friend." If your employees have no knowledge of her wrongdoing they might respond to that termination poorly.

Let me give you a real example of when leadership can focus attention on the truth and thereby strengthen your team. I had a situation where cash was disappearing out of a cash register. I knew it was happening, but couldn't figure out who was doing it, so I had a spy camera installed. Within one day, I identified the individual who was palming $20 bills, putting them in her purse and not ringing them up. On a short four hour shift she had pulled $1,000 out of the register and into her pockets. I had a detective interrogate her. He skillfully questioned her and got her to admit what she was doing. I then had her handcuffed and had the sheriff walk her out the front door of the store and off to jail.

Some of the employees were upset and I could hear them grumbling about how mean it was to embarrass her in front of all her friends. So I took the opportunity to make a comment that went something like this; I said, "Let me explain something to you. None of you are getting a raise this year, because she stole the money. I've been trying to figure out where the cash was going. I now know. She didn't just steal from me. She stole your raise. If you want to be mad at somebody, you be mad at the person that is in the back of that sheriff's car."

Instantly the attitude in the room changed. Their anger was refocused where it belonged and the attitude was very supportive of our company. Understand that there is a powerful force in nature called the leadership teaching moment. The teaching moment is that time when you need to step in and tell the truth and put things in the proper perspective. The effective use of teaching moments, is how you get a team to buy into what you're doing and to believe in your values and to engage in doing things the right way. It is such an important process that it has to be managed every day. The behavior that you model and the things that you say are critically important in whether or not your team is going to function at peak efficiency.

One more element of assembling your team is to understand the full range of people who make up your team. Your team is not just the employees that are working directly for you.

As a coach of a softball team, my team is not just the players. It's also the coaches, the parents, and the supporters of my team. As a pharmacy owner, my team is not just my employees. It is also the vendors that I count on to give me the correct product at the right time. These include my sundry vendors, my durable medical equipment vendors and my pharmacy wholesaler. It is my technology vendors who provide the management software to run the pharmacy, my interactive voice response system, my network software to keep all my computers running. It's my banker who helps me manage cash flow and manage credit card payments and manage the balance sheet of my business. It is my professional service vendors such as my accountant, my lawyer, my insurance agent, my benefit manager, my payroll management company. Every one of those suppliers is a stakeholder in my business. Selecting the correct attributes, the correct skill set, the correct values in those vendors is just as important as selecting the right employees.

Everything that I've said about hiring employees applies equally well to the rest of the players on your team. They all must be in alignment with your vision in order for your organization to run well and for your business to succeed. How do you select the right person, the right teammate, the right ancillary provider, the right vendor to help you achieve your vision and mission that will align with your values and will become a beneficial active, engaged member of your team? Not surprisingly, there are three things that you have to consider.

1. **What job** am I hiring for? Some of you might say, "That's easy. I'm hiring a technician. I'm hiring an accountant." However, there are lots of ways to do those jobs. If you want a technician that is versatile, who can do computer inputting, filling, ordering, a variety of tasks, you have to know exactly what it is that you want him or her to do. If you're hiring an

accountant, do you want the kind of person who will just send you reports and numbers? Or do you want somebody who can sit with you and talk over strategies? Knowing exactly what you're hiring for is a very critical piece of selecting the right person or vendor.

2. What do I need them to be **able to do**? So if I'm hiring for a senior-level technician, I need him or her to be able to process orders, resolve billing complaints, handle customer service complaints, know what needs to be done at the right time, be able to work the hours that I need him or her to work, be the kind of person that others look up to and help teach the younger people how to do their jobs correctly. What is it exactly that you need him or her to be able to do? If you define that and write it down, it doesn't take more than one page, it will clarify for you what you're looking for.

3. Can she do what I **need her to do**, in the **way I need it done**? Now think about this for a minute. You've defined what it is you want from a technician. You've defined what you want her to do. You want her to be able to process claims. You want her to be able to resolve claims. You want her to be able to handle customer service complaints. How is it that you want that done? Do you want it done in a perfunctory matter-of-fact manner? Do you want it done in a friendly engaging manner? Do you want it done by someone who understands her role in the workflow and will jump in and help when other people need help when the workflow gets bogged

down? Can she do the job that you need her to do, in the way that you need it done?

This is important because typically, when you're looking at a job, there are lots of people that can do the job. There are typically fewer people that can do it in the way that you want it done. There is a big difference between whether they can do it and whether they have shown in the past that they actually do it the way you want it done. When you're hiring for an entry-level job, people do not have a lot of experience, so the error rate on this decision can be fairly high. When you're hiring for a senior position in which you need people to have the skill set and ability to make an impact right away, then you're going to need to do a little more homework. It is essential to make sure they're actually capable of doing the job the way you want it done.

Let me give you an example. My wife and I decided at one point that we really needed to hire an additional pharmacist. What we wanted was a pharmacist who would take care of our customers and would relate to them well so there was no drop-off in customer service when we weren't in the pharmacy. We needed someone who had the ability to be a manager and tell people what to do and what not to do when necessary. As simple as that sounds, it was a very difficult, long process. We interviewed several people, had several people come and work a day of relief, and just couldn't really find somebody that engendered all of these qualities. This occurred over a period of about two years.

Finally I took on a new approach. Twice a week for a few months I would go spend my lunch hour in a competitor's store and watch the pharmacist work to see what they did and how they behaved. It was very easy to identify those pharmacists that I didn't want, but a couple of people came on my radar as people who had the attitude and demeanor that I was looking for. I narrowed the search to two folks. I started talking to the wholesalers that delivered there and asked what they thought. I had customers who shopped at both stores, and I would ask what they thought of this person. Eventually, I invited one of them to dinner. We sat down and we just talked and I said, "Here's what I've got going on. I just wanted to find out if maybe at some point you'd be interested in coming to work or if you know anybody that might be interested."

Well, the end result was that I hired an outstanding pharmacist who didn't know he was looking for a job. One of the problems with putting ads in the paper saying "pharmacist wanted" is that at that time the majority of pharmacists looking in the paper for a job were the ones that were out of work. The vast majority of pharmacists that couldn't find work were out of work for good reasons. Certainly this is not always true, but it was truer than not in the area of California that we were in. It was not the most ideal place where a pharmacist wanted to live, so for those that were out of work, there was a pretty good reason.

By knowing exactly what I was looking for and by scouting out and watching the person actually under real conditions and in talking to their customers, I felt fairly confident in making the job offer that I was going to get what I wanted. In any job interview, when you're talking to somebody for half an hour, it's very easy for someone to put up a good front. But then he or she doesn't always perform as advertised in the real job environment.

One compelling way to find out whether your interview impressions are accurate, if you're in a privately owned environment running your own business, would be to really take the step of asking the person to come work a couple days of relief. Interestingly enough if you have a good team of employees that are doing things the way you want to do it, you can tell after one day if that new person fits in the system or not. Your staff will tell you that he spent the whole afternoon on the computer surfing the web, trading stocks or whatever he's trying to do. They will tell you whether or not he engaged with the customers. They will tell you whether or not he seemed to know what he was doing or was accurate. It's a very inexpensive way to give up a day's wages to pay the person to come in and get an incredibly accurate depiction of how he's going to behave under fire. If you correctly define the skills and tasks that you need the new hire to be able to do, your team will evaluate whether he can do what you need him to do in the way that you need it done.

When you're in the selection process and sifting through the candidates, there are three things you should try to do. First is list the necessary knowledge, skills, abilities and attitudes that your new employee must have. Second, list the "would be nice" attributes. Occasionally, you may be surprised while interviewing that you find somebody who has a skill set that you hadn't anticipated who can add tremendous value to the team. The third issue is to be open to something that is off your list. Something that you hadn't really considered as an option may prove to have tremendous value. Great Bosses remain open to serendipity and finding something that was not on your original list when interviewing for a good employee, vendor or partner in your business.

Let me explain what I mean. Let's say that you have a pretty good baseball team. You've got a player on your team who has won the starting job at third base, and he's good, but he can also play other positions. You're searching for a second baseman because you've lost somebody or you don't have adequate skills at that job, and you find this amazingly talented third baseman. You think to yourself, "I can put him at third and move the player I already have at third to second. I'm going to upgrade two positions." That is why you need to be open to what you find. Sometimes the best hire is not the one you're looking for, but the one you find. Don't make the mistake of defining your search so narrowly that you end up overlooking a great opportunity. You need to know what your team's all about: your philosophy, your style, and your strategy. Great Bosses know and understand how their team is constructed and their strengths and weaknesses so that when they run across an opportunity, they can take advantage of it. BossHoles fill the wrong job with the wrong person.

My opinion is that when you are performing a job search and find a highly talented individual who is aligned with your philosophy, you need to hire that person. They may not fit the job that you're looking for but good people and good businesses adapt. Your organization will always benefit from adding talented, dedicated people. One possible ramification of bringing good people on is that sometimes you have to get rid of somebody that is adequate, but wasn't really as good as they needed to be. But oftentimes adding someone doesn't mean you have to subtract somebody else. Don't be afraid when you meet a highly talented person to find a way to get this person to be part of your organization. Bosses can get so immersed in the day-to-day bustle of running a business that they sometimes tolerate mediocre performance because it will be a big pain in the butt to make a change. They make excuses like we need to get through the busy season. They rationalize with ideas like she's okay, she's not horrible, but the problem is you'll never fill a hole in your team until you create one. There's always an excuse, because inertia takes over. It's easier to do nothing, sometimes. However, the impact on your team productivity is tremendous. If they know that everybody's competing for excellence and that if you don't do your job the right way, you're going to create an opening and go find somebody that can, the impact on your organization can be exhilarating. That is as long as you are also acting like a Great Boss and not a BossHole.

One of the major reasons small businesses fail is because the owner tries to do everything on their own. No one is that good. What ends up happening is the owner spends too much time doing things he doesn't like to do and isn't really good at. Instead of doing what they love the needs of the business become a burden and sap their vigor. This causes frustration, burnout and poor performance. The real secret to running a business you will love is to partner with the right people and organizations to do the parts of the business that you are not qualified for and don't want to do.

My personal philosophy is, if you do business with the best, if you do business with people that are excellent at what they do, it will benefit your organization. Good vendors are going to help you. They're going to find mistakes that you didn't find. They're going to introduce you to opportunities you didn't know were out there. They are going to help improve your organization. On the contrary, if you're cheap and hiring the least expensive person you can find very rarely are they ever going to add anything of value to your business. Here is the one question you should ask yourself when you are trying to decide whether to do it yourself or hire someone to do it for you. Would anyone else hire you to do this job? If your neighbors wouldn't hire you to do accounting, legal work, payroll or marketing why should you? I am a big believer that most services can be more useful and cost effective outsourced. A good accountant can function as the CFO of a small business and help you make investment decisions, generate monthly, quarterly, annual reports, and tax returns. She can keep you on track with your margins. She can advise you about debt structure, capital purchases, and tax strategies and provide context around important acquisitions, divestitures, and business strategies. The more she knows about you and your state of affairs, the better these accounting services can be. She can be more helpful to you in your business.

Every small business needs access to a good general counsel lawyer on occasion. If you have an employee issue, an EEOC issue or a regulatory audit issue you will need legal representation. There are lawyers who will nickel and dime you for every minute that they talk to you. There are lawyers who will work with you and won't overbill, but again, establishing a relationship before you need one is important. An experienced advisor can help you stay out of trouble rather than always trying to help you get out of trouble.

If you do your own payroll and don't keep the paperwork up to date, you can be fined and have the IRS and your state tax agency investigating you. If you fail to file a report on time you can get in big trouble. If you do your own payroll you will have absolutely no recourse, because you are the knucklehead who didn't do it right. On the other hand, there are tremendous payroll services at a very reasonable fee. They do the paperwork correctly. They keep up-to-date with the laws. They make sure your deposits are made on time. If there's any screw up, they take liability for it and they're responsible for fixing it. So for $25 to $40 a payroll period, they make sure it is done right and on time. There can be tremendous mitigation of risk by using these outside services. They help you to stay out of trouble.

The ultimate power that you have by using outsourced vendors is that if they don't do the job, you can fire them and get somebody else. It's almost always better for the small business to pay to have a good vendor helping the business perform the tasks the owner is not qualified to perform. These vendors have eyes on several other businesses and can help monitor the marketplace and stay abreast of trends. I think you get much more benefit than what you pay if you select the right partner. Just remember that building your team means selecting the right partners in addition to the right employees.

To recap the interviewing process, know what job you're hiring for, know what you need them to be able to do, and really answer the question, "Can they do what I need them to do, in the way that I need it to be done?" Great Bosses hire well by listing the attributes they want, by listing the "would be nice" attributes, and then by being open finding an opportunity to bring in somebody with an unexpected valuable skill set. Keeping that in mind, I think you will have a much better prospect of attracting and retaining the talent that you want to run your organization efficiently and become an excellent small business.

# Chapter 10: Performance on Demand

**"Coming together is a beginning; keeping together is progress; working together is success." Henry Ford**

Once you've designed your strategy, created your plan, assembled your team and selected the right members for your team, how do you get your team ready to succeed? How do you get that team that you've just assembled ready to go win that championship tournament in six months? No sports team just picks their team and goes out and wins championships. Before they can earn their way to a berth in the championship final, the journey begins with a series of actions, including basic skill development and practice. Even if you have great players who have tremendous skill sets, getting them to come together and play up to their team's ability, to learn how to play with each other, and to learn how to complement each other's skills requires practicing and trying out those skills. Even when great players from the NBA all-stars come together to play on the Olympic team they can't just throw their jerseys onto the court and win a game. There are still hours of practice and multiple game competitions required for them to hone their ability to work together as a team. They have to learn to develop offensive and defensive strategies that work with this particular assemblage of talent.

Practice has many purposes. One of them is to develop and refine your basic skills. One is to evaluate the best role for each player within your team strategy. And another purpose is to identify the gaps in your talent pool. Every practice and every pre-championship competition should improve your ability to make these three kinds of decisions. Great Bosses consistently evaluate the basic skill set of their players, the best role for each player within the team strategy and identify gaps in your talent need. If you don't use all of the pre-championship competitions correctly then you're wasting this valuable resource, this valuable practice time to create an opportunity for you to get better.

There are really only three ways to get better as a team.

1. **Enhance-** you can improve the skill performance of your existing players, that is, make every player a little bit better.

2. **Add Skills-**you can develop new skills in your existing players, like teaching them how to do stuff they didn't know how to do or they didn't know how to do together. Everyone can get better at what they do.

3. **Add/Subtract Players-** you can add new players who already have these skill sets or get rid of players that are undermining your team. There are really no other ways to improve as a team.

The toughest question for a Great Boss to answer is Is this person capable of doing it? Is she refusing to get better or has she just not been trained properly? If somebody's capable of getting better and doesn't have the right practice skills, you can teach her practice skills. If somebody is incapable of getting better no matter what you do, you're going to be wasting that valuable coaching time with somebody who just doesn't want to get better. If she doesn't have the right skills and attitude to put in the time and energy, eventually she's not going to be a good member of your team. When evaluating players who are a part of your team and you assume that everyone can get better at what she does, then there are three things that could happen.

1. This person may need **extra instruction** on what you need her to do.

2. She may need **practice** to get good at what you want her to do.

3. The third option that you have to consider, and many business people don't, is that perhaps she can develop a **new and better** way to do what you really need her to do.

Many business owners get caught up in saying, "Here's the way we do it, do it our way." Great Bosses have the guts to let their people prove them wrong. If someone actually brings a good, creative idea to the table that would make your process better, you need to have the guts to say, "You're right. Let's do it that way." Of course, there are a lot of people that think they have great ideas who don't. Or they suggest practices you've tried in the past that you know won't work. Just because you're a brand new employee with a great idea, doesn't mean that idea makes any sense. Nonetheless, a Great Boss must to be able to recognize when their staff has a better idea than they do.

Let me give you an example of this. My role in my businesses is typically the creative side, setting the agendas, and figuring out how to solve problems. Because I can't stand the maintenance chores, the day-to-day bits and pieces of droning along doing the ABCD plus X equals Y stuff. I am not very good at it and I don't even like talking about it. I mean I can do maintenance, I just feel that it is a waste of my talent. I've done it; I just get bored with it. So a lot of times, once I set the strategy up, I have to turn the details over to the people who will do that part better than I do.

If the Boss hasn't created a team of people that have the range of skill sets from the Team Dimensions profile to fact check, prioritize for you, figure out where the dead ends will come in, and to get the actual day-to-day work done, he or she can spend a lot of time pushing people down the wrong path to success. Contrast that with a situation in which you've created an environment where your team feels comfortable saying, "I hear what you're trying to do, but here's what we really do, and here's what would make it better. Here's what would get us there quicker. Here's what will allow us to do what you want only better. What you're saying will actually make it worse."

If you have a strong team of people who are comfortable disagreeing with you when they have good ideas, listen to them. Many times you will find the result to be much better than what you could have invented on your own sitting in your room. The end game for any Great Boss is to assemble the right combination of talent to be able to compete at the highest level. However, a big part of being a Great Boss is learning to modify your strategies to fit the team that you have. In addition, Great Bosses allow their teammates to express what they do well and to bring out the best of their skills by modifying and tweaking what you do to take advantage of their skill sets. BossHoles think they are always right and act like it to the detriment of team performance.

When you do field a competitive team that has the right attitudes and the right team-centered approach to things, you will inevitably compete with other teams. If your team is better trained, better at what they do, more organized, more efficient, operates using the Team Dimensions profile to solve problems, moves quicker and comes up with solutions faster, you're going to win the vast majority of the battles you get into. However, there are other good teams out there, and everybody knows that when two good teams get on the field, one team has to win and one team has to lose. That doesn't mean you're a bad team if you lose the game, and it doesn't mean they're the best team if they win the game. In any competition, the elements play out like they do and two, three, four different plays in a game can determine the final outcome when your actual competitive levels are very, very close. A couple of goofy plays can go against you, and all of a sudden you lose the game.

In any competition, there are some elements directly involved in determining the outcomes that are outside the scope of the team's control. For example, you simply cannot control the weather or the day the game is played. You cannot control the officiating. You cannot determine who your opponent is going to be in the championship game, because they have to play their games to get in too. It used to frustrate me when we'd get into a tournament, and the parents would start looking ahead in the bracket and say, "We'll beat this team and we'll beat that team and we'll be facing these guys in the championship five games later." That kind of thinking is what gets teams beat. You need to play the game you're in, you need to play it right, you need to play it hard, you need to play to win and if you win, you move forward. We don't know who we're going to play. We can't control that. All we can focus on are the things we can do to be good at what we do and give our best effort to win the game. If we win, we win. If we don't, we go fight the next one.

Great teams hope for the best, but plan for the worst. What are you going to do if you fall into the loser's bracket and have to play five games on Saturday? Do you have the pitching to fight your way out? Do you have the extra players that you need? Do you have the interchangeable pieces you need to mix and match and keep people fresh going into that last game? Well, if you just say, "We're going to win these five first games and we're going to get there," you may be unprepared to succeed if one game doesn't go your way. There is stuff that goes on that you can't control.

It takes experience and vision to train players to deal with challenges that they've never had to go through before. You need to train them to know that there are little subtle things that you need to do to be ready for something that may only happens one percent of the time, but it's going to make or break whether you win the big game or not. By the time you get in the final rounds of any major competition, the talent of your competition improves dramatically. You're not playing against the sisters of the poor anymore. The games usually get tougher, and the odds of winning continuously narrow as the talent begins to equalize and the best players, the best teams, the best organized are rising up to the top.

The team that wins is usually the team that overcame the mistakes, the injuries, and the bad breaks to outperform on the big stage. Nobody wants to be the second best pitcher on a girls fast pitch softball team when she's growing up. She knows that number one is going to get most of the innings and most all of the big games, but tournaments routinely are won because of the contributions of the number two pitcher. They frequently end up playing a big role in games that decide the tournament. If a team gets into the loser's bracket early, they can end up playing four to five games on elimination Saturday for the right to play in the championship bracket on Sunday. Then they have to beat the undefeated team twice in order to win the tournament.

Teams that don't have the depth to play five games and have enough pitching to survive Saturday are really putting themselves at a high risk of losing due to one bad inning, one close game, one bad call. So the coach's job is to clarify the roles that need to be played and get the players to embrace those roles. They must understand that the number two pitcher might never get in the game if you stay in the winner's bracket, but without that person there backing up the number one, it is a huge risk to the entire team. It's tough sometimes to get people to understand that role, because by nature everyone wants to be the starter.

Let me show you how this can play out. Our 16 and under team went to New Hampshire from California to try to win a qualifying tournament to secure a berth to the national tournament. We were able to stay in the winner's bracket all the way through the championship tournament, and we won without ever having to throw our second pitcher. My first pitcher was very good, and she was able to keep us in the winner's bracket and fight through the heat and win all the games we needed. After that tournament, my number two pitcher had not gotten into the games, and she was feeling a little down. She felt like she had not contributed to the victory. I pulled her aside and said, "You don't understand the role you played. I knew that if they beat us in the first championship game, we had the advantage, because their number one would be throwing her second game of the day, and I was going to bring you in fresh and ready to go. And you were going to shut them down. Understand that you never know when you need to be ready to carry the load, but I have full confidence that if we had to get to that second game that you were going to get the job done."

I am not sure she really believed me, but that's how the conversation went. We went to the national tournament. We got into our very first game and our number one pitcher, who was also our number four batter, severely sprained her ankle on the very first inning of the very first game. She ran down the first base line, tripped over the base went down in a heap. All of a sudden, we were in the national tournament, we hadn't thrown a pitch yet, and I had lost my number one pitcher. At that point, I looked at my number two and said, "This is what I'm talking about. I need you to step up and pitch like you've never pitched in your life, because we're counting on you to carry us through this tournament." That kid threw her lights out. She took us through five of six games. We ended up losing by one run to the team that finished second, and by one run to the team that finished third. I've never been more proud of a team in my life, the way they battled back through that adversity. The point is, she finally understood what her role was as the second pitcher.

Even if you never get to perform your on field role, it doesn't mean you're not performing a valuable service to the team. So defining what you need to be done, how you need it to be performed are things you have to understand as a Great Boss. However, it is equally important to communicate to everybody why it's important, what that role is and what they need to do throughout the course of a long year. Of course, everybody has to get their reps to stay fresh, and they have to get some practice, but when the game's on the line, that second role can be the make or break position for the entire team. Great Bosses keep everyone involved and engaged in the team while BossHoles don't. There are always jobs within each company that are more glamorous than others. There are jobs that the rank and file think are more important. But the team could not succeed without everyone's contributions and Great Bosses learn how to get everyone to understand their role and perform it with enthusiasm.

Understanding what really makes your people successful is interesting. I will give you an example. As a filling tech, for instance, there might be two technicians, one of whom is very fast and can just motor through stuff. You might think, "Wow, this person is really fast." Another person is maybe 20% slower. She's just methodical and goes at a certain pace but is deadly accurate. What you might find if you observed them closely is that the really fast person goes through bursts of really fast and bursts of really slow. The methodical person may be a bit slower but might end up producing more accurate prescriptions per hour than the other person. This accuracy takes a huge burden off the checking pharmacist. So what are you looking for? What are you paying attention to? What are you practicing? If you're noticing this person is really fast but makes mistakes because she forgets to check certain things, then she is going too fast, and that's damaging to the productivity of the workflow process. So it's important as the boss that you are paying attention to what's going on, that you're seeing what's really happening. You need to be identifying the skills as well as the flaws in skills so that when you have that overload day, you know who needs to be where and who can keep you competitive.

A Great Boss has a good practice plan. You can't just go out for three hours and run around and hit ground balls and hit fly balls and take some batting and go home. What is the purpose of your plan? What are you trying to accomplish with that practice? Are you putting people in positions where you can see if they can handle the pressure? Are you going to get them tired and then make them field ground balls so you can see how they react when they're tired? Are you going to run your drills in such a way that they don't know where the ball's going so you can guess their ability to read and react? Are you going to do read and react drills instead of just speed drills? Are you going to focus on attitude? Are you going to look at effort? Are you going to look at energy?

In getting a team ready for a championship tournament you have to practice your pre-game routine. You go through a certain order of drills and you do them for a certain reason. You get your team focused on the key skills that they will need to emphasize in the game. A properly designed pre-game plan can make the difference between winning and losing for two evenly matched teams. Let me give you an example. If we were going up against a pitcher that I know has a really nasty curveball that just snaps off at the knees on the outside corner, I'm going to work to take that pitch away from her. I want all my batters focusing on hitting the knee-high pitch on the outside corner, hard to the opposite field. I want to drill that. I don't want them trying to swing for the fences. I don't want them trying to pull the ball. I want everybody in pre-game practices hitting that ball to the opposite field, taking away the opposing pitcher's best pitch. I want all the practice pitches at the knees on the outside corner. I don't care that you can hit the home run. What I want to do is demoralize this other pitcher by taking her best pitch away from her. Great pitchers are hard to beat because they command multiple pitches. Most of the players you play against are not great pitchers.

When you do your pre-game right, when you focus on what you need to do, and you get people's mindset right and you get the readiness and you get the last-minute skills muscle memory going, you can be amazingly successful. But you can't just go through the motions. The Great Boss will not allow his or her team to give an unfocused weak effort. I will give you an example of what I mean.

There was one time at the national tournament where the girls were just acting a little silly during our pre-game routine. We had won our first few games easily and I sensed that they were beginning to take their success for granted. They were giving a halfhearted effort. I wanted them to practice bunting because my scouting reports indicated we could exploit a weakness in our next opponent. The first five or six batters got up there in pre-game practice and took weak attempts at the bunt, missed it and giggled and went on to their next station. When you watch this going on as a coach, you've got two choices. Let it go on, because they're doing the pre-game ritual, they're just not doing it right or you stop and say, "Wait a minute, that's not the way we do it." So I said, "Timeout. We're starting this all over. I'm telling you right now. You better bring up the attitude. Anybody that misses her bunt, I will pull out of the starting lineup. This is BS. We're not here to be silly. We're here to put this team away early, and we're here to get off the field and get out of the sun. I want this game over by the fifth inning. I want out of here, and I'm not accepting mediocre performance from you guys."

I reset the tone of the pre-game practice and got them to refocus and their performance immediately improved. And I know that some of you are thinking that I might have sounded like a BossHole making the threat to pull someone out of the line-up. And you would be right. The reason this worked with my team was because I rarely ever talked like that. If I did it every day it would have been demoralizing. But sometimes a Great Boss has to shock his troops to get their attention. So used very sparingly this can be effective.

The key was that I needed them to change their attitude immediately. Not only is practice important, but the way you practice is important. It's those moments when you need to step in and command respect. If you did that every single game, it would get old and it wouldn't work. But there's a time for goofing around

183

and a time for being serious. Pre-game focus is critical to performance, in my opinion. Sometimes silly and goofing around is needed when you are trying to lighten the mood after a tough loss and sometimes you need them to be serious and focused on the task at hand. A Great Boss adjusts to the needs of her team.

How does this apply to a business like pharmacy? The boss needs to monitor the mood of the team and the tension in the workplace. You need to have a good business plan. You need to have a great value strategy. You need to have the right people. You need to have them doing the right stuff. You can be easy-going and be fun-loving. But when the stuffing hits the fan and you need to get the work done, you need to be able to count on your team to get it done. There was a television program called M*A*S*H* where the doctors and nurses goofed around and got drunk and played silly pranks on each other. But the thing about M*A*S*H* that I always admired was that when the choppers carrying wounded soldiers landed, they stopped goofing around and did everything they could do to save those soldier's lives.

So in a business, the analogy is very simple. It's okay to be fun. It's okay to goof around at certain times, but when the choppers land, it's time to have everybody where they need to be, doing what they need to be doing, and doing it well. You cannot, at that moment, accept less than your best. That's what you need to have the capacity to do within your business. You need to be able to put your best, most excellent work in when it needs to be done, because that's when you earn the respect of your customers. That's when you go that extra mile. That's when you shine. That's when you outperform the competition. That's when you prove to the world that you have a fantastic operation. Never forget that when the choppers hit the ground, your team has to be prepared to do the right thing.

In order to get your people to be able to perform on demand the Great Boss must understand what good work is, train his team on how to excel, model the correct attitude and behavior, select the right teammates, refine their individual skills, and create an environment where people love to come to work. When the pressure is on, your team must be prepared to instinctively do the right thing without being told what to do at that moment. This will only happen if you have coached them to do what you want them to do, aligned their efforts with well-timed and appropriate commands, and created an environment where they strive to excel.

You will not be a perfect leader. No one was and no one is. But you can be better than 84% of your competition by just being a little above average and learning how to be a Great Boss instead of acting like a BossHole.

# At A Glance Summary

By definition, a BossHole is someone who acts like an ass and who happens to have the positional authority to impact your life. The BossHole Effect® is the powerful capacity of a BossHole to suck the joy, energy, enthusiasm and greatness out of an organization. Your challenge is two-fold. Do not tolerate BossHole behavior in others. And try not to act like a BossHole yourself.

## Chapter 1: Why Read this Book?

This book is for people who want to be Great Bosses or learn to help their not so good bosses become one. It explains the step-by-step process by which an individual can learn to be a Great Boss. Great Bosses build successful teams. Therefore, the focus of this text will be on the knowledge, skills, abilities and attitudes necessary to build a high functioning team. Real leadership occurs at unexpected times, and the moment must be seized when it occurs. You must learn to find these teaching moments, develop an effective strategy to capture the good lessons and then model the values you are trying to instill in your team.

## Chapter 2: Power of Three

In order to be a Great Boss you must understand that there are only three possible Leadership actions:

1.    Do the right thing,
2.    Do the wrong thing, or
3.    Do nothing.

So when making decisions ask yourself:

1.     Will this make it better, if so, then do it.
2.     Will this make it worse, if so, don't do it.
3.     Will this have no impact at all, if so, do something more important.

Three C's of Leadership- Great Bosses know when and where to use each mode to get the best performance from their team.

Coach Mode: building knowledge, skills and abilities in your team members.

1.     **Vision**: understand what the real endgame is.
2.     **Flexibility:** know what will work for each individual.
3.     **Process:** apply the right technique at the right time.

Command Mode: giving orders and providing direction.

1.     **Intention:** know the true message or intent of the mission.
2.     **Recognition:** learn to recognize the game you are in.
3.     **Timing:** know how to make the right call for the right conditions.

Create Mode: create an environment in which your team can thrive by providing.

1.     **Purpose:** keeping the team focused on the long-term vision for success.

2.    **Direction:** inspiring the team to excel by engaging them in the mission.
3.    **Motivation:** energizing the process of success. Provide the "why" behind the mission.

## Chapter 3: The World Is What It Is

As a leader and Great Boss you must operate in the real world not the world as you wish it to be.

Do this by avoiding:

1.    **Complacency:** when an organization becomes complacent, it stops innovating, which sows the seeds of its demise.
2.    **Complexity:** an organization begins to fail when it adds increasing layers of complexity to everything it does. These layers detract from the mission and divert resources to check list monitoring. The mission begins to get lost in the details.
3.    **Losing touch:** imagine a critical military installation that fails to provide an adequate radar shield around its base. How would the soldiers know they are in danger from an incoming threat? The worst risk an organization can take is to not have an advanced early warning system in place that identifies approaching danger.
4.    **Arrogance/Entitlement:** when an organization begins believing that it is entitled to exist regardless of performance. It begins losing touch with the reality of a dynamic marketplace.

There are only 3 types of people in the world.

1.      Those who **make things happen** and can;
        a) Become a force for improvement
        b) Become a force for destruction
        c) Waste their talent on indifference
2.      Those who **watch things happen** and can;
        a) Learn to become a leader to make good things happen
        b) earn to become a follower to help good things happen
        **c) Do nothing** and help prevent good things from happening
3.      Those who have no idea what just happened and must make one of three choices;
        a) Get educated about the **right** thing to do
        b) Get educated about the **wrong** things to do
        c) Or remain **ignorant**

To be a Great Boss, your actions must produce good results. To produce good results, you must understand what good results are and have an effective plan to achieve excellence. Effective action is the essence of good leadership. You can learn to be a good leader by mastering the three C's; Coach, Command and Create.

## Chapter 4: The Process of Leadership

The process of successful leadership requires the Great Boss to understand how to get the players to engage in the mission, to put in the work, to do the preparation and to have the attitude and effort to be successful.

Great Bosses do this by answering these important questions:

1.  What is the process by which you take a group of individuals and mold them into a highly competitive team?
2.  How do you get a group of people to get what needs to be done completed in the right way, in the right time?
3.  How do you get that team to be a group of people that energize you and are fun to be around?

There are really only three challenges you will need to master to become a Great Boss.

1.  **Clarity**: have a clear view of what it takes to win. You must learn the habits that build winning and the habits that build failure.
2.  **Process**: develop a process that builds patterns of success and does not produce fear of failure. Think twice before you speak because your words will plant the seeds of either success or failure in the mind of others.
3.  **Mindset**: internalize and accept what you can and cannot only control. You can control your team's efforts. You can control their practice habits. You can influence their attitude and effort. You cannot have any impact on the weather, the umpiring or who shows up to play against you. Worrying about things you can't control will keep you from performing to the best of your ability on the things that you can control.

Good teams are made up of good people who know that:

1.   What they do is **important**
2.   They're **good at** what they do
3.   The **boss values** their contributions to the team

## Chapter 5: Knowledge, Skills, Abilities and Attitudes

A Great Boss will:

1.   **Teach** the foundational knowledge
2.   **Develop** their skills
3.   **Reward** ability by giving your players the opportunity to demonstrate that they can perform in the real world. Don't make the decision for them. Let their play dictate the decision.

In order to determine which knowledge, skills, ability and attitudes you wish to encourage, there are three things you need to know:

1.   The key personal **success attributes** that good employees possess.
2.   The key **negative attributes** that bad employees possess.
3.   How to identify and **separate** out the good people from the bad people.

A Great Boss hires based on the answer to three questions:

1.   Does she possess the **skills** I need?
2.   Will she **mesh** well with my team?

3.  Can she do **what** needs to be done in the **way** that I need her to do it?

If one answer is no, the employer and candidate are not a match. As a Great Boss, if you compromise your standards because you have a hole to fill, you'll end up paying for it later. It is always better to wait to find the right person rather than hire the wrong one.

## Chapter 6: Awareness of What's Important

There are Three Traits of Successful Teams:

1.  **Engagement**: are team members actively, willfully, enthusiastically doing the things they need to do, or are they just going through the motions? Are they putting in their hours? Are they just complying with the letter of the law but not the spirit of what was intended?
2.  **"How to Win Awareness"** (HTWA): not everything can be covered in the policy and procedure manual. Good teams have people who know how to get things done.
3.  **Role identification:** does the person on your team perform the role they were given?

A Great Boss will generate excellent team performance based on three things:

1.  **Creating** a climate that frees good people to do the things they are capable of doing
2.  **Identifying** the abilities in good people that they don't even know they have
3.  Consistently putting good people in a **position** to succeed

A Great Boss will have good answers to several key questions.

1. Are you aware of the real performance issues?
2. Are you rewarding your people on the right metric?
3. Are your people engaged?
4. Do they solve problems or do they create them?
5. Do they know how to win?
6. Are your customers engaged and are they recommending you to their friends?
7. Are you putting people in the right roles to help your team?
8. Are your people where they can do you the most good?
9. Are you able to adjust the tone as needed to keep your team focused and energetic?
10. Are your people excited to come to work and do they get along with each other?
11. Do you know how to create the climate to free your talent, to identify the abilities of your people, and to put people in a position to succeed?
12. Do they work for you because they want to or because they need a job?

## Chapter 7: Creating Value Strategy

A critical step in developing a good business is creating a sound value strategy. You can be the best boss in the world but if your business strategy doesn't resonate with the market you will not succeed. Regardless of the business goal, successful businesses need to be able to do three things well to consistently develop and compete in the marketplace.

1. **Identify a pain in the marketplace.** What do customers say is missing? What do they want and would gladly pay for if somebody would just give it to them? Identifying this pain in the marketplace allows you to craft a strategy to fulfill that need, which will energize your growth and catapult you into a market share position.

2. **Develop a solution to remedy that pain, to ease that pain, to fill that market void.** There are lots of ways you can craft a solution for the marketplace. However, if you don't understand what the true drivers of purchase behavior are, these things are not likely to be helpful. Thus, understanding what really drives purchase behavior or the decision to buy is also critical.

3. **Make an offer to your target market.** The one piece of the puzzle that many people forget is that you have to put your offer in front of the customer. You have to offer to provide the solution that people want to have.

Once you do this you need to understand how people make choices to buy your product or shop in your store vs. others. People decide to buy a product or service based on their internal analysis of three domains:

1. **Price:** What is the price/cost in time, money, and energy for me to buy the product?

2. **Service and Benefits**: What are the services and extra benefits I get from buying the product from choice A versus choice B versus choice C?

3. **Perceived Value:** How badly do I want or need this product, and can I afford to use my limited amount of money to buy this product versus all other options I have for spending that money?

Regardless of which style of play you settle on for your business, there are three things that you have to do in order to make sure that you have the internal resources and competencies to execute your strategy.

1.  **Determine** your core values and build a strategy/style that resonates with your core values
2.  You absolutely have to **align** the style with your strengths
3.  You have to **select** the right people to be on your team

Once you have the right people on your team you should:

1.  **Understand** the strengths and weaknesses of your staff,
2.  **Place** them where they need to be to be successful,
3.  **Envision** the future. You need to be able to look downstream and say, "In order to get this to happen in a couple of months, I have to start doing stuff now that aligns with all of this," and train them to do it.

You must constantly have your finger on the pulse of your group, understand when your team is trying too hard, when they're overworked, when they're underworked, and when they're putting in the right kinds of effort. You want to encourage them and reward the strong effort. You want to immediately correct the wrong level of effort. You want to understand what's going on in your business each day and what needs to be done to make each day a success. Then you need to create an environment where everyone has the opportunity to succeed, to play their role, to do well and not with fear of failure, but with an engaged, sincere attempt to live up to your vision that you've set for your business.

## Chapter 8: Vision Mission Values

Once you've decided how you want to play, the style of play, and the style you want to run, how do you create a vision that allows you to align your daily actions with this strategy?

1. **Create that vision:** decide what is important to you, what you are good at, what you stand for, what it is that you want to achieve in the marketplace, what it is that you want to be known for.
2. **Internalize the vision.** Model the behaviors desired, document the behaviors required, demonstrate alignment with your vision, and identify which actions will create discord and confusion for your people.
3. **Apply the vision** to everything that you do in your business. If the vision is true and is good and is well thought out and is a good strategy for a successful business, then everything you do should resonate the vision.

Once you develop a vision you must do three things in order to clearly communicate it to your team:

1. **Define**: appeal to their rational minds by explaining what your vision is and why it fits in the marketplace.

2.     **Explain:** solidify the vision by appealing to the emotional side of people, which is explaining to them why it is important. Putting it in a context they cannot just understand but engage with.

3.     **Anchor:** clarify what actions you expect them to take in order to comply with the mission. All policies should be behaviorally anchored to your vision, mission and values.

Your vision and your mission must be wrapped and infused with your core beliefs. Then as a leader you use the vision, mission and values to guide your actions when using the 3 C's (Coach Command & Create).

1.     The **vision** should answer: Where do we stake our claim? Where will we achieve our greatness? What do we want to be known for?

2.     The **mission** explains: How are we going to go about doing it?

3.     The **core values** declare: What are the core principles we will use to guide our actions?

## Chapter 9: Casting Your Team of Characters

Once you've developed your strategy and you understand what a leader has to do to enforce that strategy and to lead the team to success, you are faced with the task of assembling a team to accomplish your strategy. In order to cast the right team (to include your support team such as vendors, accountant, pay rolls, lawyers, etc.) you must:

1.     **Understand** what the **attributes** are that you are looking for in a teammate that will enable you to enact your strategy then:

a) Hire people you know already have these attributes or

b) Hire people and train them to do these things

c) Identify the Attitude, Effort and Character that you expect from your people.

2. **Identify** the "knockout" or **unacceptable** behaviors and attributes that you absolutely don't want on your team.

3. Consider problem solving style- create a well-rounded team by understanding whether someone is a Creator, Advancer, Refiner, Executor or Flexor and how that will fit into your current group.

When in doubt give them a two-week trial period. If they can't display the skills, abilities, attitude, effort and character you need by then, then they are unlikely ever to be able to. Then keep your people by reminding them that what they do is important, that they're good at it and that you value their contributions to the team.

When you actually get ready to hire you need to identify three things:

1. What **job** am I hiring for?

2. What do I **need** them to be able to do?

a) Create a list of must have's (skills, abilities, attitudes, etc.)

b) Create a list of "would be nice's"

c) Be open to something that is off your list

3. Can she do **what** I need her to do, in the **way** I need it done?

# Chapter 10: Performance on Demand

Once you've designed your strategy, created your plan, assembled your team and selected the right members for your team, how do you get your team ready to succeed? How do you get that team that you've just assembled ready to go win that championship tournament in six months? There are really only three ways to get better as a team.

1. **Enhance**- you can improve the skill performance of your existing players, that is, make every player a little bit better.
2. **Add Skills**-you can develop new skills in your existing players, like teaching them how to do stuff they didn't know how to do or they didn't know how to do together. Everyone can get better at what they do.
3. **Add/Subtract Players**- you can add new players who already have these skill sets or get rid of players that are undermining your team. There are really no other ways to improve as a team.

When evaluating players who are a part of your team and you assume that everyone can get better at what she does, then there are three things that could happen.

1. This person may need extra **instruction** on what you need her to do.
2. She may need **practice** to get good at what you want her to do.
3. The third option that you have to consider, and many business people don't, is perhaps she can

develop a **new and better** way to do what you really need her to do.

Great teams hope for the best, but plan for the worst. It takes experience and vision to train teams to deal with challenges that they've never had to go through before. You need to train them to know that there are little subtle things that you need to do to be ready for something that may only happen one out of 100 times, but it's going to make or break whether you win the big game or not.

In order to get your people to be able to perform on demand the Great Boss must:

1. Understand what good work is
2. Train his team on how to excel
3. Model the correct attitude and behavior
4. Select the right teammates
5. Refine their individual skills and
6. Create an environment where people love to come to work

When the pressure is on, your team must be prepared to instinctively do the right thing without being told what to do at that moment. This will only happen if:

1. You have **Coached** them to do what you want them to do
2. Aligned their efforts with well-timed and appropriate **commands** and
3. **Created** an environment where they strive to excel.

You will not be a perfect leader. No one was and no one is. But you can be better than 90% of your competition by learning how to be a Great Boss and not acting like a BossHole.

# About the Authors

## Greg L. Alston

Greg L. Alston is an Associate Professor of Pharmacy Management and Assistant Dean for Assessment at Wingate University School of Pharmacy in North Carolina. He has a unique resume of management success. He graduated cum laude with a Doctor of Pharmacy degree from the University of the Pacific while simultaneously becoming a credentialed K-12 teacher through the School of Education. During his years in the chain drug industry he was the first in his graduating class promoted to pharmacy manager, and was the first pharmacist to become corporate training manager, marketing manager and general category manager on the buying staff for Sav-on Drugs. He went on to become a Regional Pharmacy Manager for Thrifty Drugs and the California Regional Pharmacy Manager for Smith's Food and Drug. After 15 years in the chain drug industry he founded and operated Draculas Castle Halloween shops and Best Pharmacy and Medical Supply in Southern California.

During his business career he has supervised thousands of employees, worked for hundreds of bosses, and battled organizational stupidity at every turn. After selling the healthcare businesses in 2007 he "retired" to become the Assistant Dean for Assessment at Wingate University School of Pharmacy and within 18 months earned the National Award for Excellence in Assessment from the American Association of Colleges of Pharmacy in 2009. He currently teaches Pharmacy Management, Community Health Outreach and

Pharmacy Communications Skills courses and frequently consults with corporate clients and individual pharmacists looking to solve their most perplexing problems.

He began coaching Girls Fastpitch softball when his daughter Valerie began playing in 1991. Teams he helped coach reached the national tournament finals for their age bracket, nine times in 10 years with eight top ten finishes, including two national championships. Dr. Alston draws on his experience as a teacher, pharmacist, leader, boss, coach, parent, iconoclast and occasional BossHole to demystify the process of becoming a Great Boss. He and his high school sweetheart, June, have been married for 36 years, and jointly raised two children, seven dogs, and innumerable employees. He has an uncanny ability to communicate complex subject matter in clear and simple terms and has been known to not only call a spade a spade, but to occasionally refer to it as a F**KING shovel.

You can follow him at his blog:
www.GregLAlston.com

## Valerie R. Alston

Valerie R. Alston is the type of daughter that everyone would be proud to have. She was an excellent student earning high school valedictorian and numerous other honors. She was a gifted athlete earning national titles, state championships, a major college athletic scholarship and several other individual awards. But more importantly she is a calm, competent competitor, a loyal teammate, a natural empath, an enthusiastic teacher, an unconditional friend, an intuitive leader and only an occasional DaughterHole. After spending 48 weekends per year playing, talking and living fastpitch softball with Coach Greg she has pretty much taught him everything he knows about how to be good at what he does. Her wisdom, experience and guidance permeate every page of this book.

Valerie Alston has been a Master Resilience Trainer-Performance Expert with the Army's Comprehensive Soldier and Family Fitness Program since 2008. She earned her B.S. in Kinesiology while playing college softball for the University of Minnesota. After 15 years of playing and competing in softball at the National Level she fell in love with the mental and emotional side of performance and earned a Master's Degree in Sport Psychology from Boston University. Building on her experiences as an elite athlete and her education she has spent the past five years traveling all over the world working with and training Soldiers and their families how to use mental skills, to be at their best, when it matters the most. She is a Certified Consultant with the Association of Applied Sport Psychology. Valerie draws on her experience as an athlete, exposure to good and bad leaders, her training in Sport Psychology and her work with the military to define good leadership and drive optimal performance.

## Acknowledgements

No effort of this magnitude is done without help. But enumerating the long list of people that helped me develop the story I have told you in this book would take more pages than I have available. For those of you who will see yourself woven within a thread of this narrative. I am honored to have you in my life. For those of you that would have preferred I didn't bring you in to the narrative I am pleased to disappoint you. But there is one person who deserves special mention because she provided the ability to get this project off the ground. Without her support and incredible ability to translate my spoken words in to typed English sentences that make sense I would still be pecking away on my laptop trying to bang this out. So I need to send a quick shout out to Juli Inhofer, my baby sister. When we were kids we made up our own language based on Pig Latin so, Hey Dadle Ping Badle Uv U-lay Madle !

# THE TEN THINGS

## A NEW MANAGER MUST GET RIGHT FROM THE START!

## Managing People Simplified

DR. GREG L. ALSTON
VALERIE R. ALSTON MA

# Chapter One: Introduction

## I'm a Manager, Now What?

Every day somewhere in the world a person is starting a new job as a new manager of a department, a work unit, a business or an organization. Regardless of the level of experience you have in your previous job, nothing truly prepares you to take on an entirely new job in management. Management is different than non-management work. The big difference is that you are now responsible for the work of others. Others will look to you for guidance and support, decisions and policy. There is nothing more exhilarating than getting your first promotion. And there is nothing more frightening than having to manage people. People come in all shapes and sizes and have a wide variety of motivations. It can be a challenging task to get any group of people to work together as a team. However, ultimately your success as a manager is going to depend on your ability to get a group of people to do good work on behalf of your organization.

So while you are excited about getting a promotion, somewhere in the back of your mind a little voice usually begins to say, "I hope I don't blow it." It is perfectly normal to be a little bit nervous when you are taking on a task that you have never done before.

Regardless of your own level of personal confidence, there is always an element of uncertainty when you move in to a new job or a new role. But as someone who has done this 30 or 40 times over the course of my last 40 years in business, I hope you will let me share with you some of the ways you can make this transition easier and more likely to be successful.

To emphasize that I actually know what I am talking about I wish to tell you a story about one of the times when I made the transition to a new management job. This particular event happened to me after I had more than 10 years of experience in management and I was able to deal with it satisfactorily because of that experience. But as I am telling this story, simply imagine what this would have been like if this was your very first foray into being a manager.

In 1990 I was hired by the Vice President of Pharmacy at Thrifty Drug Stores in Southern California to take over as the pharmacy manager of the Beverly Hills location. This location was one of the top five stores in the chain for prescription volume but was being poorly managed. Because the vice president and I had worked together at a previous company, he trusted me to take over this high-volume location. However, because I had not worked for Thrifty Drug in the past I had not been trained on their prescription dispensing software and systems. For those of you who have never worked in a pharmacy, essentially everything that the work team in a pharmacy does requires them to use the prescription dispensing software to input prescriptions, print labels, fill prescriptions and counsel patients on their medications. No two pharmacy systems are identical and they frequently use entirely different terminology and short codes to operate. I was scheduled to take over as pharmacy manager on Monday morning and was to meet with the former pharmacy manager for orientation half-an-hour before the store was scheduled to open. I arrived 45 minutes early and got the key to the pharmacy from the store manager and let myself in to get the lay of the land. The store was scheduled to open at 9 o'clock.

At 8:45, the first pharmacy technician showed up to work but no pharmacist appeared. At 9 o'clock, I was still the only pharmacist in the building and customers were congregating in front of the pharmacy so we opened. Monday mornings are usually the most hectic times in a community pharmacy. And this Monday was no exception. Instantly 40 to 50 customers were in line waiting to fill prescriptions. The problem was the pharmacist who was supposed to show up to orient me to the software never did. The technicians were never told how to turn on the pharmacy computers, so while they knew how to use the software they had no idea how to boot up the computers. I know this is difficult for you to understand in the modern age but at those times the computer was a huge 4 x 4 foot box housed in the basement of the building and many people did not own computers at home so not everyone possessed knowledge about how to use computers like they do now. By 9:15, I was able to figure out how to power up the computers but I still had no idea how to operate the system. The crowd of customers had grown and was beginning to get unruly.

So here is a brief synopsis of my first day as a new manager at this drugstore in Beverly Hills. I had no training in the systems. I had never met the people that I was going to be working with. The people that were supposed to train me never showed up. The operation was so poorly run that the staff was not trained to do their jobs without supervision. And the customers in the waiting area were pretty much ready to fight each other. I had four clerks and two technicians standing there staring at me looking for guidance that would a) help them to do their jobs and b) keep them from getting yelled at. My first temptation was to simply lock the door and leave. After all, who could expect anyone to operate effectively as a manager under those conditions? But then my professional training and management experience kicked in and I formulated a plan, took action and not only survived the day, but earned the respect of my fellow employees and customers.

I am not going to tell you exactly what I did yet because I want to ask you this simple question. What would you have done? You can see what I did at the end of Chapter Six. If you have the ability to create a clearly formulated plan that would work to defuse this situation and develop your team into an effective business unit, then you probably don't need to read this book. If you are less certain that you would've been able to handle the situation then I suggest that you continue reading.

The first step in achieving success in your new role as a manager is to admit to yourself that you do not know everything you need to know right now. The second step will be to seek out advice from those who have gone through this before you so that you can learn from others' mistakes without having to make them all yourself.

The purpose of this book is not to teach you everything you need to know about management. That task will take years and multiple experiences before you consider yourself a truly great boss. However, there are a few simple secrets that you can learn that will help you avoid the mistakes that other new managers have made and put you into the right frame of mind to be a successful boss right from the beginning.

This book is intentionally short. As an author and college professor I have found that I am much more successful at helping students learn a skill when I focus on one problem and offer one solution at a time. The clarity of purpose and the brevity of the discussion make it much easier for someone to recognize what they are doing wrong, identify what they can do to fix it, and take the actions necessary to perform well.

So here's what I suggest that you do. (1) Carve out some quiet time to read this book through in its entirety. The chapters are organized in a way that should help you think about the things you'd need to do successfully to be a good manager. (2) While you are reading this book keep a notepad and pencil by your side. When something you read resonates with your particular situation make a note of the chapter and page and why this resonates with you. (3) After you are done reading, create a list of the top three things you are going to do differently to become an excellent new manager.

There is an iconic scene in the movie, _The Iron Lady_ starring Meryl Streep as Margaret Thatcher when she is being interviewed by a physician in the hospital. The doctor is trying to determine whether she has slipped into a state of dementia when he asks her, "How are you feeling?" Mrs. Thatcher responds by chastising the doctor for caring more about feelings than thoughts and ideas. She then launches into a monologue that I believe is well worth repeating. If you prefer to see the YouTube video you can watch this movie clip at the following link:http://youtu.be/GSXYHqs0KPo

"Watch your thoughts because they become your words. Watch your words because they become your actions. Watch your actions because they become your habits. Watch your habits because they become your character. And watch your character because it becomes your destiny. What we think is what we become."

These are powerful words that describe the logic behind a successful "leadership" mindset. I think the most important thing that you need to do when you're taking on this new role of management is to truly understand how your thoughts and actions will become the performance of your team. With that in mind this short book is designed to help you understand the essentials of managing people. This book will focus on the big picture and a few of the core themes critical to good management and leadership practices. If you would like a more detailed description of the process involved in taking a group of people and turning them into a championship caliber team, you may want to read my more detailed description of this process in the best-selling book, *The BossHole Effect: Managing People Simplified*, which is available on Amazon and Barnes & Noble. In addition you can visit, **www.theBossHoleeffect.com** or you can furthermore go to the following site **www.GregLAlston.com** for more information about all of the books in the Managing People Simplified Series.

The first chapter of this book will deal with describing the essence of what employees expect from their boss. The second chapter will deal with what your company or organization expects from you as the manager of your business unit. The third chapter will point out the top 10 mistakes that new bosses frequently make. The fourth chapter will focus on the mental framing required for you to be successful as a manager.

And the fifth chapter will describe the most important steps you can take right away to hit the ground running and set yourself up to be successful.

As you read this book I would ask you to do me two favors. If you think of a question that this book does not answer sufficiently to make you feel comfortable taking on this role as a manager, would you please write it down and email it to me? My main concern in writing this book is that the information I am providing you is useful. Without your feedback I will never know. So please go to the following page on my blog and leave a comment for me. I will read them and respond to the best of my ability. **www.GregLAlston.com/questions**

Secondly, I would ask that after you read this book would you please go on to **Amazon.com** via your account that you used to buy the book and write a brief review providing your honest opinion of the quality and usefulness of the book. Your review will help others decide whether or not to buy the book but it will also help me determine whether I have framed the message correctly for the audience for which I intended it. With so much junk being written and published these days, I want to assure you that I am a real person with real experiences that has done everything I talk about and who genuinely has your interest at heart. I want to make sure that I am helping you succeed. So please take a few minutes after you have read the book to write a short review.

If you enjoy this subject matter and would like to join my Google+ community for people interested in Management and Leadership you can find the Community at *Management and Leadership Simplified* by searching for Google plus communities.

www.ingramcontent.com/pod-product-compliance
Lightning Source LLC
Chambersburg PA
CBHW071118280326
41935CB00010B/1045